HANDBOOK
of GOVERNMENT
&
PUBLIC SERVICE
CAREERS

edited by Annette Selden

VGM Career Horizons
a division of *NTC Publishing Group*
Lincolnwood, Illinois USA

Library of Congress Cataloging-in-Publication Data

VGM's handbook of government and public service careers / edited by Annette Selden.

    p.   cm.
ISBN 0-8442-4142-3
1. Civil service positions—United States. I.Selden, Annette. II. VGM Career Horizons
(Firm)
JK716.V46 1993
353.001'03—dc20
                                            92-11255
                                                CIP

Published by VGM Career Horizons, a division of NTC Publishing Group.
©1994 by NTC Publishing Group, 4255 West Touhy Avenue,
Lincolnwood (Chicago), Illinois 60646-1975, U.S.A.

3 4 5 6 7 8 9 0 VP 9 8 7 6 5 4 3 2 1

Contents

Contents

How to Use This Book

VGM's Handbook for Government and Public Service Careers contains vital information on 47 popular careers in government and public service. Each career has been carefully researched and described in text that is easy to understand. The careers are listed in alphabetical order for easy reference, and each is described in the following fashion:

◊ *The Job.* A general description of what the job is like and what persons in the field are expected to do.

◊ *Places of Employment and Working Conditions.* Where major employers in the field are located and what type of work environment to expect, i.e., office work, outdoor work, urban location, rural location. Typical working hours are also given.

◊ *Qualifications, Education, and Training.* How to qualify for a job in the field, what type of education is necessary, and any special training that may help you get a start in the field.

◊ *Potential and Advancement.* The approximate number of persons employed in the field nationwide, projections on whether the field will grow or shrink in the upcoming years, and typical paths of advancement for workers.

◊ *Income.* The most current salary figures available, for beginners in the field and for experienced workers. Keep in mind that such figures are subject to change, due primarily to supply and demand within the labor force and to inflation. Be sure to check with various employers and associations for the most recent figures while conducting your job search.

◊ *Additional Sources of Information.* Names and addresses of associations and other groups that can supply more information about careers in the field. These organizations can be very helpful, so be sure to contact them if you need additional information.

This handy reference book allows you to compare and contrast various careers in government and public service, all within one volume. You can use it to find out about fields that may already interest you, or you can read it cover to cover in order to explore a variety of career paths that you might find appealing.

Accountant

The Job Accountants maintain records of how much money a government agency spends and receives. They prepare and analyze the financial reports that furnish up-to-date information for government agencies. Because the financial condition of an organization influences just about every government decision, the data accountants provide is very important.

Government accounting is one of four major fields of accounting. The other three are public, management, and internal auditing. Government accountants work at the federal, state, and local levels. They ensure that money is received and spent in accordance with laws and regulations. They also maintain and examine the financial records of government agencies and audit the records of businesses and individuals whose financial activities are subject to government regulations.

Many government accountants are certified public accountants (CPAs), who hold a certificate issued by the state board of accountancy. To obtain certification they usually must be college graduates, but a few states allow the substitution of a certain number of years of experience for the educational requirement. They also must pass the CPA examination prepared by the American Institute of Certified Public Accountants.

Beginners in accounting usually start as ledger accountants, junior internal auditors, or as trainees for technical accounting positions.

Related jobs are budget officer, financial analyst, tax collector and revenue agent, and FBI special agent.

Places of Employment and Working Conditions All government organizations use the services of accountants. Accountants work for the smallest municipal governments as well as for the government of the United States. Many accountants work as internal revenue service agents or in financial management, financial institution examination, and budget administration.

Many government accountants work for auditing agencies such as the Air Force Audit Agency, the Defense Contract Audit Agency, the Navy Audit Agency, and the General Accounting Office. Others work in the government departments of Agriculture, Treasury, Health and Human Services, and Energy.

Accountants have desk jobs and generally work between 35 and 40 hours a week. Many work longer hours, particularly during the tax season. Some travel may be required for accountants who perform audits at government facilities.

1

Qualifications, Education, and Training   If you want to be an accountant, you need an aptitude for mathematics. In addition, you must be neat, accurate, able to work with little supervision, and able to handle responsibility.

Training in accounting is available at business schools and correspondence schools as well as at colleges and universities. For beginning accounting positions in the federal government, four years of college (including 24 semester hours in accounting or auditing) or an equivalent combination of education and experience is required.

Work experience is important and can help an applicant get a job after graduation. Therefore, many colleges provide students with an opportunity to gain experience through internship programs while still in school.

Accountants who wish to advance professionally must continue studying accounting throughout their careers. Seminars and courses are offered by many professional associations. More and more accountants are studying computer operation and programming in addition to accounting subjects.

More and more states are requiring CPAs to complete continuing education courses for license renewal.

Potential and Advancement   The demand for skilled accountants is expected to increase rapidly through the year 2005 as government agencies continue to grow in size and complexity.

Beginning accountants often start as cost accountants, junior internal auditors, or as trainees for other accounting positions. As they rise through the ranks, they may advance to accounting manager, chief cost accountant, budget director, or manager of internal auditing.

Income   In the federal government, salaries for all accountants average about $40,000 a year. Junior accountants and auditors begin at about $17,000; those with superior academic records can start as high as $21,000. A beginner with a master's degree or two years of experience starts at $25,700.

Additional Sources of Information
American Institute of Certified Public Accountants
1211 Avenue of the Americas
New York, NY 10036

National Society of Public Accountants and the Accreditation Council
   for Accountancy and Taxation
1010 North Fairfax Street
Alexandria, VA 22314

The Institute of Internal Auditors
249 Maitland Avenue
Altamonte Springs, FL 32701

Aerospace Engineer

The Job Designing, developing, testing, and producing aircraft, missiles, and spacecraft are the duties of aerospace engineers. This work is important to national defense and to the space program.

Aerospace engineers often specialize in one area such as structural design, instrumentation and communication, or production methods. They may also specialize in one type of product such as helicopters, passenger planes, or rockets.

The Department of Defense and the National Aeronautics and Space Administration, as well as other federal government agencies, provide one out of ten jobs in this field.

Places of Employment and Working Conditions

Most federally employed aerospace engineers are with the National Aeronautics and Space Administration, the Air Force, and the Navy. Jobs are scattered throughout the country.

Some aerospace engineers work in offices all of the time while others work in laboratories and industrial plants or at construction sites. Some are required to travel a great deal to plants or construction sites.

Qualifications, Education, and Training

The ability to think analytically, a capacity for details, and the ability to work as part of a team are all necessary. Good communication skills are also important.

Mathematics and the sciences must be emphasized in high school. A bachelor's degree in engineering is the minimum requirement in this field. In a typical curriculum, the first two years are spent in the study of basic sciences such as physics and chemistry and mathematics, introductory engineering, and some liberal arts courses. The remaining years are usually devoted to specialized engineering courses.

Engineering courses can last from four to six years. Those that require five or six years to complete may award a master's degree or may provide a cooperative plan of study plus practical work experience with a nearby industry.

Because of rapid changes in technology, many aerospace engineers continue their education throughout their careers. A graduate degree is necessary for most teaching and research positions and for many management jobs. Some persons obtain graduate degrees in business administration.

All states require licensing of engineers whose work may affect life, health, or property or who offer their services to the public. Those who are licensed, about one-third of all engineers, are called registered engineers. Requirements for licensing include graduation from an accredited engineering school, four years of experience, and an examination.

To qualify for an entry-level position with the federal government, applicants must have graduated from a school of engineering, must be registered as a professional engineer, must have completed 60 hours in an engineering curriculum, and must have one year of professional experience or have passed the written test required for professional registration or the Engineer-in-Training examination administered by the Board of Engineering Examiners in each state.

Potential and Advancement   Employment in this field is expected to grow about as fast as the average through the year 2005. However, a large proportion of aerospace engineering jobs are defense related, so employment with the federal government will be limited because Defense Department expenditures for military aircraft, missiles, and other aerospace systems are expected to decline.

Income   The average yearly salary for engineers employed by the federal government is about $49,367.

Additional Sources of Information

Accreditation Board for Engineering and Technology
345 East 47th Street
New York, NY 10017

American Institute of Aeronautics and Astronautics, Inc.
AIAA Student Programs
The Aerospace Center
370 L'Enfant Promenade, SW
Washington, DC 20024

American Society for Engineering Education
11 Dupont Circle
Suite 200
Washington, DC 20036

Junior Engineering Technical Society (JETS)
1420 King Street
Suite 405
Alexandria, VA 22314

National Society of Professional Engineers
1420 King Street
Alexandria, VA 22314

Society of Women Engineers
345 East 47th Street
Room 305
New York, NY 10017

Agricultural Cooperative Extension Service Worker

The Job   Extension agents, as they are usually called, are employed jointly by state land-grant universities and the U.S. Department of Agriculture. They conduct educational programs for rural residents in agriculture, home economics, youth activities, and community resource development. Agents usually specialize in one of these areas, and most of them are employed at the county level.

Extension agents usually work with groups of people. An agent for youth activities conducts 4-H meetings and organizes recreational activities such as camping. An agent specializing in home economics would present programs and information on nutrition, food preparation and preservation, child care, and home furnishings. In community resource development, an extension agent would help local community leaders plan public projects such as water supply and sewage systems, recreational programs, libraries, and schools. Agricultural science extension agents conduct seminars for local farmers and provide advice to individual farmers who have specific problems.

Extension agents use every available communication method to reach as large an audience as possible. They write for local newspapers, appear on local radio and television stations, and sometimes produce films covering specialized subjects.

Some extension agents are employed at the state level at land-grant universities where they coordinate the work of the county agents. State extension agents often conduct research and may spend part of their time teaching classes at the university.

County extension service workers also work in home economics, child care, and health services.

Places of Employment and Working Conditions
Extension agents work in rural areas throughout the United States.

Most extension service offices are located in small communities, a fact that appeals to people who do not wish to work in the city. Extension agents lead a very busy, active life and, depending on specialty area, may spend a great deal of time outdoors. Many meetings and seminars are presented in the evening for the convenience of the participants.

Qualifications, Education, and Training
Extension workers must have the ability to work with people and be interested in farm life.

A bachelor's degree in an appropriate specialty is the basic requirement for extension service agents. Some training in communication skills and teaching techniques is extremely valuable. Agents usually receive specific training in extension work in a preinduction training program and may improve their skills through regular in-service training programs.

In most states, specialists and state-level or multicounty agents must have a graduate degree, sometimes a Ph.D.

Potential and Advancement
There are about 15,000 cooperative extension workers. The number of workers will grow very slowly through the year 2000 to between 16,000 and 17,000.

Agents at the county level can advance to positions as state specialists. State specialists can then be promoted to administrative positions in the state extension service. Some workers with the necessary advanced degrees move on to staff positions at a college or university.

Income
Salaries vary by locality and depend on the education and experience of the worker. Starting salaries range from $11,500 to $16,500 a year, and workers with experience average about $21,000 a year.

Additional Sources of Information

Extension Service
U.S. Department of Agriculture
Room 1080
South Building
Washington, DC 20250

Air Traffic Controller

The Job   The safe and efficient operation of the nation's airways and airports is the responsibility of air traffic controllers. They coordinate all flight activities to prevent accidents. Some regulate airport traffic; others regulate planes in flight between airports.

Airport traffic controllers monitor all planes in and around an airport. Planes that are not visible from the control tower are monitored on a radar screen. When the airport is busy, controllers fit the planes into a holding pattern with other planes waiting to land. The controller must keep track of all planes in the holding pattern while guiding them in for landings and instructing other planes for takeoffs.

After a plane departs the airport, the airport traffic controller notifies the appropriate en route controller. There are 24 en route control centers in the United States where en route controllers work in teams of two or three. Each team is assigned a specific amount of airspace along one of the designated routes generally flown by all airplanes.

Before taking off, each pilot files a flight plan that is sent by teletype to the appropriate control center. When a plane enters a team's airspace, one member of the team will communicate with the pilot by radio and monitor the flight path on radar. This controller will provide information on weather, nearby planes, and other hazards, and can approve and monitor such things as altitude changes.

All civilian air traffic controllers work for the Federal Aviation Administration (FAA). Military and naval air installations use their own personnel as air traffic controllers, and many civilian controllers acquire their skills during military service.

Places of Employment and Working Conditions   Air traffic controllers work at civilian and military installations throughout the country, but most of them work at major airports and air traffic control centers near large cities.

Because control towers and centers operate around the clock, seven days a week, controllers work night and weekend shifts on a rotating basis. They work under great stress, because they usually have several planes under their control at one time and decisions they make affect the safety of many people.

Qualifications, Education, and Training
Potential controllers need a decisive personality since they must make quick decisions, and they should be articulate since instruction to pilots must be given immediately and clearly. A quick and retentive memory is a must as is the ability to work under pressure and to function calmly in an emergency.

Air traffic controller trainees are selected through the federal civil service system. Applicants must be under 31 years of age, in excellent health, and have vision correctable to 20/20. They must pass a written examination that measures their ability to learn and their aptitude for the work. In addition, applicants must have three years of general work experience or four years of college or a combination of both. Applicants with experience as military controllers, pilots, or navigators can improve their test rating by scoring well on the occupational knowledge portion of the examination. Passing a drug screening test is also required of applicants.

Trainees receive 11 to 13 weeks of intensive on-the-job training combined with formal training. They learn the fundamentals of the airway system, federal aviation regulations, aircraft performance characteristics, and the use of controller equipment. Their training also includes practice on simulators at the FAA Academy in Oklahoma City.

After training, it usually takes several years of progressively more responsible work experience to become a fully qualified controller.

A yearly physical examination is required of all controllers, and they must pass a job performance examination twice a year. Drug screening is also a condition of continued employment.

Potential and Advancement
There are about 32,000 air traffic controllers.

Competition for air traffic controller jobs will be stiff through the year 2005; the number of applicants is expected to exceed the number of openings. Employment in this field is expected to grow more slowly than the average for all occupations through the year 2005. The need for air traffic controllers will be reduced because of the introduction of a new air traffic control system that will involve the use of a computer radar network. This network will perform many of the tasks now performed by air traffic controllers.

Controllers can advance by transferring to different locations and larger airports. In installations with a number of air traffic controllers, experienced controllers can advance to supervisory positions. Some advance to management jobs in air traffic control or to administrative jobs in the FAA.

Income   The average salary for controllers is about $47,200 a year. Beginners earn about $21,000 a year.

Depending on length of service, controllers receive 13 to 26 days of paid vacation and 13 days of paid sick leave each year; they also receive life insurance, health benefits, and a retirement program. Because of the stress of this occupation, the retirement program is more liberal than for other federal employees.

Additional Sources of Information   A pamphlet on air traffic controllers is available from any U.S. Office of Personnel Management Job Information Center. To find the telephone number of your local Job Information Center, look in your telephone book under U.S. Government, Office of Personnel Management. If there is no listing in your telephone book, dial the toll-free number 800-555-1212 and request the number of the Office of Personnel Management Job Information Center in your area.

Budget Analyst

The Job   The research and analysis performed by budget analysts result in financial plans that determine how a government agency can spend its funds and what the extent of its future operations will be. A government agency oversees many different programs, and it is the budget analyst's responsibility to advise and assist in the establishment of a budget that will most efficiently distribute funds among these programs.

Budget analysts' work begins when the heads of various programs or departments submit their budget proposals, which include information such as proposed increases, estimated costs and expenses, and the funds necessary to finance the program. Analysts review these proposals, making sure that they are complete and accurate. They also compare the proposed budget with past and current budgets. A government agency is allotted a certain amount by Congress, and the analysts must make sure that the agency as a whole does not spend more than that amount.

After reviewing the various proposals, analysts submit a preliminary budget to the agency head, explaining their reasons for allowing or denying certain funding requests. At this point, they work together with the agency head, analyzing the proposed budget and developing alternate plans where necessary. After the budget has been fine-tuned, it must be approved by the agency head.

Analysts are not finished once a budget has been approved. Throughout the rest of the year, they must monitor the budget by reviewing reports and accounting records to make sure that funds are being used in the manner in which they were designated. They may make suggestions for the use of excess funds and recommend program cuts where deficits occur. They monitor the funds for different programs and inform program heads of their availability.

Analysts play a part in the development of procedural guidelines and policies that govern the development and maintenance of a budget.

Places of Employment and Working Conditions Budget
analysts work for almost every government agency, with the largest agencies employing the greatest number. More than one-third of the analysts employed by the government work in Washington, D.C. Of those employed by the federal government, seven out of ten work for the Department of Defense.

Budget analysts usually work in an office about 40 hours a week. They may come under more pressure during those times when they are developing budgets and performing midyear and final reviews of budgets. During these periods, they often are required to work more than 40 hours.

Budget analysts usually work alone, but they are often expected to attend meetings and training sessions. Some travel may be involved.

Qualifications, Education, and Training Budget analysts
must have strong analytical skills and an aptitude for mathematics, statistics, and computer science. They must be able to work well with others and function effectively under pressure and strict time constraints. Oral and written communication skills are important for presenting budget proposals.

Most government agencies consider only applicants who have at least a bachelor's degree in accounting, finance, or economics.

The federal government offers extensive on-the-job and classroom training to entry-level analysts. Classes include budget formulation; budget execution; federal budget process; and planning, programming, and budget systems. Analysts are encouraged to take classes throughout their careers.

Potential and Advancement   There are about 21,000 budget analysts employed by federal, state, and local governments. Employment is expected to grow about as fast as the average for all occupations through the year 2005. Competition will be keen because of the increasing number of qualified applicants. Those with a college degree, especially a master's, will have the best opportunities.

Beginning analysts usually work under close supervision. It usually takes one or two years to achieve an intermediate-level position and a few more years to be promoted to a senior-level position.

In the federal government, entry-level analysts begin with tasks such as comparing projected costs with prior expenditures; consolidating and entering data prepared by others; and assisting more experienced analysts by researching regulations governing budget practices. As they progress, they develop and formulate budget estimates and justification statements, perform in-depth analyses of budget requests, write statements supporting funding requests, and advise program managers of the status and availability of funds.

Income   In the federal government, entry-level analysts earn $16,900 a year. Those with a master's degree or at least one year of financial experience begin at $21,000. The average salary for analysts employed by the federal government is about $35,000 a year.

Additional Sources of Information

U.S. Office of Personnel Management
1900 E Street, NW
Washington, DC 20415

Chemist

The Job   Chemists perform laboratory research to gain new knowledge about the substances that make up our world. Knowledge gained in basic research is then put to practical use and applied to the development of new products. Their research also leads to the development of energy-saving and pollution-reducing processes. Chemists have made many advances in medicine, agriculture, and other areas.

Chemists often specialize in one of the subfields of chemistry. *Analytical chemists* study the structure, composition, and natures of substances. *Organic chemists* study all elements made from carbon compounds, which include vast areas of modern industry. The development of plastics and many other synthetics is a result of the work of organic chemists. *Inorganic chemists* study compounds other than carbon and are involved in the development of such things as solid-state electronic components. *Physical chemists* study energy transformation and are engaged in finding new and better energy sources.

Chemists are the largest group of scientists working for the federal government. They work primarily in health and agriculture and in federal agencies, including the departments of Defense, Health and Human Services, and Agriculture. They are also employed by state and local governments in the areas of health and agriculture.

Places of Employment and Working Conditions   Chemists work in all parts of the country, primarily in industrialized areas.

Chemists usually work in modern facilities in laboratories and offices. There are some hazards in working with certain chemicals, but there is little risk if proper procedures are followed.

Qualifications, Education, and Training   The student who plans a career as a chemist should enjoy performing experiments and building things and should have a genuine liking for math and science. A wide range of abilities is necessary, including perseverance, concentration on detail, good eye-hand coordination, and the ability to work independently.

High school students looking forward to a career in chemistry should take as many math and science courses as possible and develop good laboratory skills. Foreign language courses can also prove valuable.

Many colleges and universities offer a bachelor's degree in chemistry. Courses include analytical, organic and inorganic, and physical chemistry, as well as mathematics and physics.

A master's degree in chemistry, usually requiring extensive, independent research, is offered by several hundred colleges and universities. Independent research is required for master's and Ph.D. degrees.

Potential and Advancement   The outlook for employment is good primarily because the problems of pollution, energy, and health care must be addressed by chemists in government agencies. Employment of chemists in

crime detection work is also expected to increase on local, state, and federal levels.

In all areas, a Ph.D. will continue to be the key to advancing to administrative and managerial positions.

Income   Chemists employed by the federal government earn an average of $46,847 a year.

Additional Sources of Information

American Chemical Society
Career Services
1155 16th Street, NW
Washington, DC 20036

CIA Worker

The Job   The Central Intelligence Agency (CIA) gathers and analyzes information from all over the world that might affect the interests of the United States. This information is used by the government's senior policy makers as they make decisions on U.S. policy concerning many issues and areas.

In addition to employing those who gather information, the CIA employs intelligence analysts, economists, geographers, and other specialists in science and technology to provide additional information on foreign countries and governments. Career fields within the CIA include computer sciences, economics, engineering (especially mechanical, electrical, aerospace, nuclear, and civil), foreign area studies, languages, mathematics, photographic interpretation, the physical sciences, psychology, and library science.

The CIA career development program provides orientation, training, opportunities for growth, and advancement in specialty fields as well as in general intelligence work.

A full range of clerical positions is also available with the Central Intelligence Agency, including some overseas assignments.

Places of Employment and Working Conditions   Most CIA
employees work in the Washington, D.C., area, but some positions require for-

eign travel or assignment for varying lengths of time. Overseas tours of duty are optional for clerical personnel and usually last for a two-year period.

The usual workweek is 40 hours, but this may vary depending on specialty field and area of assignment.

Qualifications, Education, and Training
General qualifications for anyone interested in working for the CIA include good character, intelligence and resourcefulness, willingness to accept responsibility, and a strong motivation for public service. Applicants should be willing to serve overseas if necessary and be aware that their work must often remain anonymous. U.S. citizenship is required.

An undergraduate or graduate degree in an appropriate field is necessary; related work experience is a plus. Some colleges and universities take part in a cooperative education program with the CIA. Interested undergraduates who are majoring in engineering, physics, mathematics, computer science, business administration, or accounting may spend part of their time in a cooperative work program.

Applicants for clerical positions must meet the basic requirement for specific jobs and must complete an aptitude test.

A background security investigation will be completed on all accepted applicants before assignment to duty. Because this investigation takes time, applicants should apply well in advance of the time they wish to start working.

Potential and Advancement
Although the CIA employs a wide variety of people in many fields, active recruitment of specific specialties varies from year to year. Information on current job opportunities is available from the CIA; see listings at the end of this article.

The CIA offers advancement opportunities to all employees. Formal and on-the-job training is available during early and midcareer stages, and professional-level training is given not only within the CIA but also at other government training establishments and at local colleges and universities. The CIA has its own highly regarded Language Learning Center for employees who wish to study a foreign language.

For clerical employees, the CIA's Office of Training offers courses in administrative procedures, writing, employee development, and supervision and management. Off-campus courses are offered by some local universities and specialized schools at the CIA headquarters building; tuition costs for approved job-related courses are paid by the CIA. Foreign language training is provided for those who are to serve overseas.

Income   Because this agency's function is to gather information crucial to the nation's security, it is cloaked in secrecy. Certain information, such as the amount of its budget, is not a matter of public record. Employees of the CIA are not a part of the civil service pay system administered by the Office of Personnel Management, but their pay and benefits are claimed to be similar to other government workers.

Additional Sources of Information   If you are in college, see your placement officer and request an interview with the CIA representative who visits your campus from time to time or whose regional office may be situated nearby.

Write to the Central Intelligence Agency, Office of Personnel, Washington, D.C. 20505; (703)482-1100. Enclose a resume of your education and experience and ask for preliminary application forms.

City Manager

The Job   A city manager, usually appointed by the elected officials of a community, administers and coordinates the day-to-day activities of the community. The city manager oversees such functions as tax collection and disbursement, law enforcement, public works, budget preparation, studies of current problems, and planning for future needs. In a small city, the manager handles all functions; in a larger city, the manager usually has a number of assistants, each of whom manages a department.

City managers and their assistants supervise city employees, coordinate city programs, greet visitors, answer correspondence, prepare reports, represent the city at public hearings and meetings, analyze work procedures, and prepare budgets.

Most city managers work for small cities (under 25,000) that have a council-manager type of government. The council, which is elected, hires the manager, who is then responsible for running the city as well as for hiring a staff. In cities with a mayor-council type of government, the mayor hires the city manager as his or her top administrative assistant.

A few managers work for counties and for metropolitan and regional planning bodies.

Most city managers begin as management assistants in one of the city departments such as finance, public works, or planning. Experience in several different departments is valuable and can provide a well-rounded background.

This is a new and growing profession with room for people with training in a variety of disciplines that relate to the functions and problems of urban life.

Places of Employment and Working Conditions City managers are employed throughout the country in cities of all sizes, but job opportunities are greatest in the eastern states.

Working conditions for a city manager are usually those of an office position with considerable public contact. More than 40 hours a week is usually required, and emergency situations and public meetings frequently involve evening and weekend work.

Qualifications, Education, and Training Persons planning a career in city management must be dedicated to public service and willing to work as part of a team. They should have self-confidence, be able to analyze problems and suggest solutions, and should function well under stress. Tact and the ability to communicate well are very important.

A graduate degree is presently required for most entry-level positions in this field. An undergraduate degree in a field such as engineering, recreation, social work, or political science should be followed by a master's degree in public or municipal administration or business administration.

Requirements in some of the 185 colleges and universities that offer advanced degrees in this field include an internship of six months to a year, in which the candidate must work in a city manager's office to gain experience.

Potential and Advancement Approximately 11,000 people are presently employed as city managers, and the field is growing rapidly. However, job competition is expected to be very strong over the next few years, due to an increase in the number of graduates in this field.

Recent computerized management techniques for taxes, traffic control, and utility billing will create openings for those trained in finance, while an increased emphasis on broad solutions to urban social problems will result in opportunities for those with a strong public administration background. Also, the council-manager system of government is the fastest growing type in the country, and the move is toward professional, rather than elected, city management.

Generally, a beginner in this field starts as an assistant to a city manager or department head, with promotions leading to greater responsibility. A city manager will probably work in several different types and sizes of cities in his or her career, which will further broaden the person's experience and promotion potential.

Income   Salaries for city managers depend on education, experience, job responsibility, and the size of the employing city. Salaries are generally high; the average annual salary is over $57,000. Salaries range from $33,000 a year in towns with populations of fewer than 2,500, to $125,000 in cities of more than a million.

Benefits usually include travel expenses and a car for official business.

Additional Sources of Information

International City Management Association
777 North Capitol Street, NE
Suite 500
Washington, DC 20002

Civil Engineer

The Job   The is the oldest branch of the engineering profession. Civil engineers design and supervise construction of buildings, roads, harbors, airports, dams, tunnels and bridges, and water supply and sewage systems. Those employed by the federal government plan military bases, roads, and dams.

Specialties within civil engineering include structural, hydraulic, environmental (sanitary), transportation, geotechnical, and soil mechanics. Many civil engineers are in supervisory or administrative positions. They may supervise a construction site or administer a large municipal project such as highway or airport construction.

Over 40 percent of all civil engineers work for federal, state, and local government agencies.

Places of Employment and Working Conditions   Civil engineers work in all parts of the country, usually in or near major industrial and commercial centers. Some work in foreign countries.

The largest federal government employer of civil engineers is the Army Corps of Engineers, which employs about 6,000. Other major employers include the Department of Transportation and its Federal Highway Administration, the Department of Agriculture, the Navy, and the Department of the Interior.

A great deal of a civil engineer's time is spent outdoors. Civil engineers sometimes work in remote areas and may have to move from place to place as they work on different projects.

Qualifications, Education, and Training   The ability to think analytically, a capacity for details, and the ability to work as part of a team are all necessary. Good communication skills are important.

Mathematics and the sciences must be emphasized in high school.

A bachelor's degree in engineering is the minimum requirement in this field. In a typical curriculum, the first two years are spent studying the basic sciences such as physics and chemistry and mathematics, introductory engineering, and some liberal arts courses. The remaining years are usually devoted to specialized engineering courses. Engineering programs can last from four to six years. Those requiring five or six years to complete may award a master's degree or may provide a cooperative plan of study plus practical work experience in a nearby industry.

Because of rapid changes in technology, many engineers continue their education throughout their careers. A graduate degree is necessary for most teaching and research positions and for many management jobs. Some persons obtain graduate degrees in business administration.

Engineering graduates usually work under the supervision of an experienced engineer or in a company training program until they become acquainted with the requirements of a particular company or industry.

All states require the licensing of engineers whose work may affect life, health, or property or who offer their services to the public. Those who are licensed, about one-third of all engineers, are called registered engineers. Requirements include graduation from an accredited engineering school, four years of experience, and a written examination.

Potential and Advancement   Over 79,000 civil engineers work for federal, state, and local government agencies. Job opportunities should be very good, as employment is expected to grow faster than the average for all occupations through the year 2005.

Civil engineers will be in demand to meet the needs of a growing population. They will design and construct higher capacity transportation, water supply, and pollution control systems; large buildings; and other structures. Already existing roads, buildings, and other public structures will require repair or replacement, creating many employment opportunities for civil engineers.

Income   The average yearly salary for engineers employed by the federal government is about $49,367.

Additional Sources of Information

Accreditation Board for Engineering and Technology
345 East 47th Street
New York, NY 10017

American Society of Civil Engineers
345 East 47th Street
New York, NY 10017

American Society for Engineering Education
11 Dupont Circle
Suite 200
Washington, DC 20036

Junior Engineering Technical Society (JETS)
1420 King Street
Suite 405
Alexandria, VA 22314

National Society of Professional Engineers
1420 King Street
Alexandria, VA 22314

Society of Women Engineers
345 East 47th Street
Room 305
New York, NY 10017

Computer Programmer

The Job   Computer programmers write detailed instructions, called programs, that list the orderly steps a computer must follow to solve a problem. Once programming is completed, the programmer runs a sample of the data to make sure the program is correct and will produce the desired information. This is called debugging. If there are any errors, the program must be changed and rechecked until it produces the correct results. The final step is the preparation of an instruction sheet for the computer operator who will run the program.

A simple program can be written and debugged in a few days. Those that use many data files or complex mathematical formulas may require a year or more of work. On such large projects, several programmers work together under the supervision of an experienced programmer.

Programmers usually work from problem descriptions prepared by systems analysts, who have examined the problem and determined what steps are necessary to solve it. In organizations that do not employ systems analysts, employees called programmer-analysts handle both functions. An applications programmer then writes detailed instructions for programming the data. Applications programmers usually specialize in business or scientific work.

A systems programmer is a specialist who maintains the general instructions (software) that control the operation of the entire computer system.

Beginners in this field spend several months working under supervision before they begin to handle all aspects of the job.

A leader in the development of computers, the federal government is the largest single user of computer systems.

Places of Employment and Working Conditions
Programmers are employed in all areas of the country. Major federal government employers include the departments of the Treasury, Defense, and Health and Human Services; however, nearly every government agency employs programmers.

Most programmers work a 40-hour week, but they don't always work from 9 to 5. They may occasionally work on weekends or at other odd hours to have access to the computer when it is not needed for scheduled work.

Qualifications, Education, and Training
Patience, persistence, and accuracy are necessary characteristics for a programmer. Ingenuity, imagination, and the ability to think logically are also important.

High school should include as many mathematics courses as possible.

There are no standard training requirements for programmers. Depending on the work to be done, an employer may require only some special courses in computer programming; a college education; or a graduate degree in computer science, mathematics, or engineering.

Computer programming courses are offered by vocational and technical schools, colleges and universities, and junior colleges. Home-study courses are also available, and a few high schools offer some training in programming.

Scientific organizations require college training; some require advanced degrees in computer science, mathematics, engineering, or the physical sciences.

Because of rapidly changing technologies, programmers take periodic training courses offered by employers, software vendors, and computer manufacturers.

Like physicians, they must keep constantly abreast of the latest developments in their field. These courses also aid in advancement and promotion.

Potential and Advancement
This is a rapidly growing field because of the expanding use of computers. Simple programming needs will be increasingly handled by improved software, so programmers with only the most basic training will not find as many job openings as in the recent past. A strong demand will continue, however, for college graduates with a major in computer science or a related field.

There are many opportunities for advancement in this field. Programmers may be promoted to lead programmers with supervisory responsibilities. Both applications programmers and systems programmers can be promoted to systems analyst positions.

Income
In the federal government, beginning programmers with a college degree or qualifying work experience earn about $17,000 a year; those with superior academic records begin at $21,000.

Additional Sources of Information

Data Processing Management Association
505 Busse Highway
Park Ridge, IL 60068

American Federation of Information Processing Societies
1899 Preston White Drive
Reston, VA 22091

Association for Computing Machinery
11 West 42nd Street
New York, NY 10036

Correction Officer

The Job   Correction officers, more commonly known as prison guards, are responsible for the daily activities of prisoners. They guard prisoners both inside and outside the prison. They explain prison rules to inmates and listen to their complaints and needs.

Inside the prison, correction officers escort inmates to their daily activities, such as meals, classes, work, and chapel. If a prisoner is sick, the correction officer sees that he or she gets to the hospital. Correction officers oversee recreational activities and make sure that all bars, gates, doors, and windows are secure so that prisoners cannot escape. They must count the prisoners at certain times during the day and report any that are missing. Correction officers must intervene in the case of a fight, disturbance, or escape attempt. They must also make sure prisoners do not have any forbidden articles.

Some correction officers oversee prisoners outside the boundaries of the prison. They escort prisoners to and from jobs and on court-ordered trips, and return escapees and parole violators.

Places of Employment and Working Conditions   Most correction officers work in state and county correctional institutions. Some work in federal prisons.

Correction officers usually work a 40-hour week. Since prisons must be guarded around the clock, some guards work nights, evenings, and weekends.

Correction officers may find themselves in dangerous situations at times. They must be able to remain calm and make good decisions quickly.

Qualifications, Education, and Training   Correction officers must be U.S. citizens and, in most states, at least 21 years old.

A high school education is necessary or preferred for most jobs. Some two-year colleges offer programs in correctional science.

Most states test applicants on their ability to read and follow directions. Other states give a civil service examination. Some states require a psychological examination, and all require a physical exam.

All beginning officers must go through a training program lasting from one to six months. Trainees learn modern correctional methods, personal defense, physical restraint of prisoners, and the use of guns.

Potential and Advancement
The job outlook for correction officers is very good through the year 2005. Opportunities will result from the expansion of existing prisons and the construction of new ones.

As they gain additional training, experience, and education, correction officers advance in rank and salary. They move from correction officer to sergeant to lieutenant to correction captain to deputy keeper. Titles for ranks may vary from institution to institution. They may also transfer to related areas, such as probation and parole.

Income
Pay scales vary by rank and by the employing branch of the government. Correction officers working for the federal government start at a salary of about $18,900 a year; supervisory correction officers, at $25,700. The average salary for federally employed correction officers is $23,800; supervisory correction officers, about $27,400.

State-employed correction officers average about $22,900 annually. Beginning officers earn average starting salaries of $18,400; annual starting salaries range from $12,400 in Kentucky to $29,400 in California. Average salaries for experienced officers range from $14,700 in South Dakota to $37,400 in New Jersey.

Additional Sources of Information

The American Correctional Association
8025 Laurel Lakes Court
Laurel, MD 20707

American Jail Association
P.O. Box 2158
Hagerstown, MD 21742

American Probation and Parole Association
P.O. Box 51017
Salt Lake City, UT 84152

Criminologist

The Job   The field of criminology broadly covers all those who work in law enforcement, criminal courts, prisons and other correctional institutions, and those employed in counseling and rehabilitation programs for offenders. Many jobs in these categories are covered elsewhere in this book. This job description, however, focuses on the term *criminologist* as it applies to those who are involved in scientific investigation of crime through analysis of evidence.

The scientific gathering, investigation, and evaluation of evidence is known as criminalistics, and those who work in this field are called forensic scientists. These technical experts, including specially trained police officers and detectives, carefully search the victims, vehicles, and scenes of crimes. They take photographs, make sketches, lift fingerprints, make casts of footprints and tire tracks, and gather samples of any other relevant materials.

Once the evidence has been gathered, scientists and technicians trained in various natural sciences analyze it along with reports from medical examiners and pathologists. Other specialists interview victims to prepare composite pictures or psychological profiles of the criminal. Those who specialize in firearms and ballistics conduct tests to identify weapons used in specific crimes.

Forensic specialists also include handwriting experts, fingerprint and voiceprint specialists, polygraphy (lie detector) examiners, and odontologists (teeth and bite-mark specialists).

Almost all people in this field work for federal, state, or local law enforcement and investigative agencies. Municipal and state police departments all have investigative responsibilities that include the processing of evidence. Some employ civilian scientists and technicians, but many utilize specially trained police officers in police crime laboratories.

Related jobs are chemist, medical laboratory technologist, biochemist, and police officer.

Places of Employment and Working Conditions   Criminologists work primarily for law enforcement agencies in state and local government. The federal government employs forensic scientists in a number of agencies, including the Federal Bureau of Investigation and the Secret Service.

Forensic scientists may be on call at all hours and may be required to work out-of-doors or in unpleasant conditions when gathering evidence.

Qualifications, Education, and Training   Personal traits of curiosity, ability to work with detail, patience, and good eyesight and color vision are necessary.

High school should include mathematics and science courses.

College training depends on the specialty field selected. A degree in chemistry, biology, electronics, or other appropriate field should be obtained. Course work in forensic science is offered by some colleges and by law enforcement training programs and police departments.

Potential and Advancement
Demand is expected to be strong for criminologists as their expertise is important to the reduction of legally and socially deviant behavior. Job opportunities will be best for those with a Ph.D.

Income
In the federal government, beginning criminologists with a bachelor's degree earn annual starting salaries of about $17,000, and those with a superior academic record, $21,000. For those with a master's degree, the starting salary is about $25,700 a year; with a Ph.D., about $31,100.

Experienced criminologists employed by the federal government earn an average annual salary of about $49,600.

Additional Sources of Information

American Society of Criminology
1314 Kinnear Road
Suite 212
Columbus, OH 43212

Applicant Recruiting Office
Federal Bureau of Investigation
10th and Pennsylvania Avenue, SW
Washington, DC 20520

Economist

The Job   Economists study and analyze the relationship between the supply and demand of goods and services and how they are produced, distributed, and consumed. Economists perform research, observe and monitor economic trends, develop economic forecasts, and collect and analyze data. They study topics such as energy costs, inflation, imports, exports, interest rates, and employment.

Economists employed by the government prepare studies to assess economic conditions and the need for changes in government policies. They study the products people buy and the costs of those products. They determine how large the supply of products is. This information allows economists to regulate prices and develop policies that will enable the economy to grow. They usually work in the fields of agriculture, business, finance, labor, transportation, and international trade and development.

Places of Employment and Working Conditions   Economists work in all large cities. The largest concentrations are in the New York City, Washington, D.C., and Chicago metropolitan areas. Some economists work abroad for the Department of State and other U.S. government agencies. The largest federal employers of economists are the departments of State, Labor, Agriculture, and Commerce.

Government economists typically have structured work schedules. They may work alone, conducting research and writing reports, or they may work as part of a team. Economists sometimes face deadlines and are required to work overtime to meet them. Some travel may be required.

Qualifications, Education, and Training   Anyone interested in this career field should be able to work accurately and in detail since economics entails careful analysis of data. Good communications skills are also necessary.

High school should include as many mathematics courses as possible.

A college major in economics is the basic preparation for a career in economics. Students should also study political science, psychology, sociology, finance, business law, and international relations. A bachelor's degree is sufficient for many beginning research, administrative, management trainee, and sales jobs. However, graduate school is increasingly necessary for many positions and for advancement.

Potential and Advancement   Growth in the economics field is expected to be about as fast as the average for all occupations through the year 2005. Most opportunities will occur as workers transfer to other occupations or leave the labor force for some reason.

There will be keen competition for economist positions. Opportunities will be better for those with a master's degree and best for those with a Ph.D.

Advancement in this field usually requires advanced degrees.

Income   The federal government offers average starting salaries of $17,000 a year to applicants with a bachelor's degree; to those with a bachelor's degree and a superior academic record, $21,000; to those with a master's degree, $25,700; to those with a Ph.D., $31,100; and to those with experience, $37,300.

Experienced economists employed by the federal government earn an average salary of $50,100 a year.

Additional Sources of Information

American Economic Association
1313 21st Avenue, S.
Nashville, TN 37212

Electrical and Electronics Engineer

The Job   Electrical and electronics engineering is the largest branch of engineering. These engineers design and develop electrical and electronic equipment and products. They may work in power generation and transmission; machinery controls; lighting and wiring for buildings, automobiles, and aircraft; computers; radar; communications equipment; missile guidance systems; or consumer goods such as television sets and appliances. Most of the electrical and electronics engineers employed by the federal government are concerned with communications equipment.

Engineers in this field usually specialize in a major area such as communications, computers, or power distribution equipment, or in a subdivision such as aviation electronic systems. Many are involved in research, development, and design of new products; others in manufacturing and sales.

Places of Employment and Working Conditions   Major

federal employers of electrical and electronics engineers are the armed forces, the National Aeronautics and Space Administration, and the Coast Guard.

Many engineers work in laboratories or at construction sites while others work in an office all the time. A few engineers are required to travel extensively. Many engineers work 40 hours a week, but deadlines may bring extra pressure to the job.

Qualifications, Education, and Training   The ability to think

analytically, a capacity for detail, and the ability to work as part of a team are all necessary. Good communication skills are important.

Mathematics and the sciences must be emphasized in high school.

A bachelor's degree in engineering is the minimum requirement in this field. In a typical curriculum, the first two years are spent in the study of basic sciences such as physics and chemistry and mathematics, introductory engineering, and some liberal arts courses. The remaining years are usually devoted to specialized engineering courses. Engineering programs can last from four to six years. Those requiring five or six years to complete may award a master's degree or may provide a cooperative plan of study plus practical work experience with a nearby industry.

Because of rapid changes in technology, many engineers continue their education throughout their careers. A graduate degree is necessary for most teaching and research positions and for many management jobs. Some persons obtain graduate degrees in business administration.

Engineering graduates usually work under the supervision of an experienced engineer or in a company training program until they become acquainted with the requirements of a particular company or industry.

All states require licensing of engineers whose work may affect life, health, or property or who offer their services to the public. Those who are licensed, about one-third of all engineers, are called registered engineers. Requirements include graduation from an accredited engineering school, four years of experience, and a written examination.

Potential and Advancement   Increased demand for computers,

communications, and military electronics is expected to provide ample job opportunities for electrical engineers through the year 2005. A sharp rise or fall in government spending for defense could bring about a greater or lesser demand for workers in this field.

Income The average annual salary for engineers employed by the federal government is about $49,367.

Additional Sources of Information

Accreditation Board for Engineering and Technology
345 East 47th Street
New York, NY 10017

American Society for Engineering Education
11 Dupont Circle
Suite 200
Washington, DC 20036

Institute of Electrical and Electronics Engineers
United States Activities Board
1828 L Street, NW
Suite 1202
Washington, DC 20036

Junior Engineering Technical Society (JETS)
1420 King Street
Suite 405
Alexandria, VA 22314

National Society of Professional Engineers
1420 King Street
Alexandria, VA 22314

Society of Women Engineers
345 East 47th Street
Room 305
New York, NY 10017

Employment Counselor

The Job   Employment counselors, also called vocational counselors, help jobseekers who have difficulty finding jobs. They provide services to experienced workers who have been displaced by automation or who are unhappy in their present jobs and to returning veterans, school dropouts, handicapped and older workers, former prisoners, and those with minimal job skills.

In-depth interviews, aptitude tests, and other background information help the counselor evaluate the capabilities of each person. The counselor then helps the jobseeker develop a vocational plan and a job goal that will be implemented using whatever remedial action is necessary. This could include education or retraining, physical rehabilitation or psychological counseling, specific work experience, or development of appropriate work skills. Once the jobseeker obtains a position, the counselor usually provides follow-up counseling for a period of time.

Counselors must be familiar with the local labor market and with the job-related resources of the community. Some employment counselors contact local employers and keep abreast of job openings within local industries to refer jobseekers to specific jobs.

Most employment counselors work for state employment centers or community agencies. Others work for private agencies, prisons, training schools, and mental hospitals. Employment counselors working for the federal government have jobs with the Department of Veterans Affairs and the Bureau of Indian Affairs.

Places of Employment and Working Conditions   Employment counselors work throughout the country in communities of all sizes.

Counselors usually work a 40-hour week. Those in community agencies may work overtime or some evening and weekend hours.

Qualifications, Education, and Training   Anyone interested in this field should have a strong interest in helping others, should be able to work independently and keep detailed records, and should possess patience.

Graduate work beyond a bachelor's degree or equivalent counseling-related experience is necessary for even entry-level jobs in employment counseling. Undergraduate work should include courses in psychology and sociology; graduate work includes actual counseling experience under the supervision of an instructor.

Employment counselors working for state and local government agencies must fulfill local civil service requirements, which include specific education and experience requirements and a written examination.

Potential and Advancement   The employment outlook for employment counselors is not as good as it is for counselors working in other areas. Employment opportunities in federal and state agencies will depend on the availability of government funding.

Employment counselors in federal and state agencies may advance to supervisory or administrative positions.

Income   Median annual earnings for employment counselors are $31,000. The middle 50 percent earn between $24,200 and $40,000 a year. Those at the top of the pay scale earn over $49,300 a year, and those at the bottom earn less than $17,700 a year.

Additional Sources of Information

American Association for Counseling and Development
5999 Stevenson Avenue
Alexandria, VA 22304

State employment services offer information about job openings and entrance requirements.

Environmentalist

The Job   Pollution is one of the major problems facing modern society. Environmentalists are workers who find ways to control and prevent water, air, and land pollution. They must keep in mind the needs of the environment as well as the economic needs of industries.

There are several areas of specialization for environmentalists: land conservation, acid rain, toxic waste removal and disposal, wildlife preservation, and groundwater contamination. Environmentalists do research, perform environmental impact studies, and develop systems to monitor pollution. Some work with community groups and leaders to solve environmental problems in a particular area. They may attend public meetings or appear before legislative committees or in court.

Some environmentalists work as consultants. They are hired by the government or a private company to study a problem and advise their employer on how best to deal with it in order to protect the environment and not suffer financial loss.

Other environmentalists work with members of Congress and state legislatures to see that laws are written and passed that protect the environment.

Places of Employment and Working Conditions
Environmentalists may work for the federal government, usually in the Environmental Protection Agency (EPA) or the Department of the Interior. Others work for state and local governments. Employers hiring environmentalists also include environmental consulting firms, nonprofit environmental organizations, chemical and oil companies, and mining companies.

Environmentalists work indoors, in an office, as well as outdoors. They often have to travel to problem sites to perform research and studies. Their work hours may be irregular.

Qualifications, Education, and Training
Environmentalists must be able to work well with people. They should be good communicators and have an interest in the outdoors and science.

Environmentalists usually must have a bachelor's degree in one of the environmental or natural sciences. Some have degrees in engineering or political science. Most environmentalists continue to take courses in order to stay aware of the latest developments in the field.

Potential and Advancement
Environmentalists will be in demand through the year 2005. Because of current awareness of environmental problems and the subsequent laws that are being passed to regulate environmental quality, companies will need the advice of experts in the field. This should result in very good opportunities for environmentalists.

Environmentalists usually begin as researchers or interns. They advance by becoming project directors or managers. Those with experience often become consultants.

Income   Salaries for beginning environmentalists average about $17,000 to $21,000 a year. Experienced environmentalists earn between $31,000 and $42,000 or more annually.

Additional Sources of Information

Association of Environmental Scientists and Administrators
3433 Southwest McNary Parkway
Lake Oswego, OR 97035

National Association of Environmental Professionals
P.O. Box 9400
Washington, DC 20016

FBI Special Agent

The Job   Special agents for the Federal Bureau of Investigation (FBI) investigate violations of federal laws in connection with bank robberies, kidnappings, white-collar crime, thefts of government property, organized crime, espionage, and sabotage. The FBI, which is part of the U.S. Department of Justice, has jurisdiction over many different investigative matters. Special agents, therefore, may be assigned to any type of case, although those with specialized training usually work on cases related to their background. Agents with an accounting background, for example, may investigate white-collar crimes such as bank embezzlements or fraudulent bankruptcies or land deals.

Because the FBI is a fact-gathering agency, its special agents function strictly as investigators, collecting evidence in cases in which the U.S. government is, or may be, an interested party. In their casework, special agents conduct interviews, examine records, observe the activities of suspects, and participate in raids. Because the FBI's work is highly confidential, special agents may not disclose any of the information gathered in the course of their official duties to unauthorized persons, including members of their families. Frequently, agents must testify in court about cases that they investigate.

Although they usually work alone on most assignments, two agents or more are assigned to work together when performing potentially dangerous duties such as arrests and raids. Agents communicate with their supervisors by radio or telephone as the circumstances dictate.

Places of Employment and Working Conditions

Most agents are assigned to the FBI's 59 field offices located throughout the nation and in Puerto Rico. They work in cities where field office headquarters are located, or in resident agencies (suboffices) established under field office supervision, to provide prompt and efficient handling of investigative matters arising throughout the field office territory. Some agents are assigned to the Bureau headquarters in Washington, D.C., which supervises all FBI activities.

Special agents are on call 24 hours a day and must be available for assignment at all times. Their duties call for some travel, for they are assigned wherever they are needed in the United States or Puerto Rico. They frequently work longer than the typical 40-hour week.

Qualifications, Education, and Training

To be considered for appointment as an FBI special agent, an applicant usually must be a graduate of a state-accredited law school; a college graduate with a major in accounting, engineering, or computer science; or be fluent in a foreign language.

Applicants for the position of FBI special agent must be citizens of the United States; between 23 and 35 years old; and willing to serve anywhere in the United States and Puerto Rico. They must be capable of strenuous physical exertion and have excellent hearing and vision, normal color perception, and no physical defects that would prevent their using firearms or participating in dangerous assignments. All applicants must pass a rigid physical examination as well as written and oral examinations testing their aptitude for meeting the public and conducting investigations. All of the tests except the physical examinations are given by the FBI at its facilities. Background and character investigations are made of all applicants. Appointments are made on a probationary basis and become permanent after one year of satisfactory service.

Each newly appointed special agent is given about 15 weeks of training at the FBI Academy at the U.S. Marine Corps base in Quantico, Virginia, before assignment to a field office. During this period, agents receive intensive training in defensive tactics and the use of firearms. In addition, they are thoroughly schooled in federal criminal law and procedures, FBI rules and regulations, fingerprinting, and investigative work. After assignment to a field office, the new agent usually works closely with an experienced agent for about two weeks before handling any assignments independently.

Potential and Advancement   The jurisdiction of the FBI has expanded greatly over the years. Although it is impossible to forecast personnel requirements, employment may be expected to increase with growing FBI responsibilities.

The FBI provides a career service, and its rate of turnover is traditionally low. Nevertheless, the FBI is always interested in applications from qualified persons who would like to be considered for the position of special agent.

All administrative and supervisory jobs are filled from within the ranks by selection of those agents who have demonstrated the ability to assume more responsibility.

Income   The entrance salary for FBI agents is about $28,300 a year. Experienced agents start at around $44,300 a year, and supervisory agents start at around $52,400.

Additional Sources of Information

Applicant Recruiting Office
FBI
10th and Pennsylvania Avenue, SW
Washington, DC 20520

Firefighter

The Job   Firefighters must be prepared to respond to a fire and handle any emergency that arises. This is dangerous work that requires courage and expert training.

Firefighting requires organization and teamwork. Each firefighter at the scene of a fire has specific duties assigned by a company officer; but each must also be ready to perform any of the duties—such as connecting hoses to hydrants, positioning ladders, or operating pumps—at any time, because duties change in the course of a fire. Firefighters may also be called on to rescue people or to administer first aid.

Between fires, firefighters spend their time cleaning and maintaining equipment, carrying out practice drills, and maintaining their living quarters. They also take part in fire prevention activities such as building inspections and educational programs for schools and civic groups.

Over 90 percent of all firefighters work for municipal fire departments. The remainder work on federal and state installations or in private firefighting companies.

Most firefighters are members of the International Association of Firefighters (AFL-CIO).

Places of Employment and Working Conditions

In some cities, firefighters are on duty for 24 hours and then off for 48 hours. In other cities, they work a 10-hour day shift or a 14-hour night shift, with shifts rotated frequently. The average workweek varies from 42 to 52 hours, but some firefighters work as many as 84 hours a week. These duty hours usually include free time which can be used for personal interests or study.

Firefighters face the risk of injury or death in the course of their work and must work outdoors in all kinds of conditions and weather.

Qualifications, Education, and Training

A firefighter must have courage, mental alertness, physical stamina, mechanical aptitude, and a sense of public service. Initiative, good judgment, and dependability are essential. Because firefighters live together as well as work together, they should be able to get along with others.

Applicants for municipal firefighting jobs may have to pass a written test and medical examination that includes a test that screens for drug use and test of strength, physical stamina, and agility. They must meet other local regulations as to height and weight, have a high school education or equivalent, and be at least 18 years old. Experience as a volunteer firefighter or firefighting training received in the armed forces improve the applicant's chances for appointment to a job, and some communities also give credit to veterans of the armed forces.

Beginners are usually trained at the city's fire school for several weeks and are then assigned to a fire company for a probationary period.

Fire departments frequently conduct training programs to help firefighters upgrade their skills, and many colleges offer courses such as fire engineering and fire science that are helpful to firefighters. Experienced firefighters also continue to study to prepare for promotional examinations.

Potential and Advancement

There are about 280,000 firefighters. Employment of firefighters is expected to increase about as fast as the average through the year 2005. There will be considerable competition for the jobs, and the number of applicants will be greater than the number of job openings. Turnover of firefighting jobs is relatively low.

Opportunities for promotions are good in most fire departments. Promotion to lieutenant, captain, battalion chief, assistant chief, deputy chief and finally chief depend on written examination, seniority, and rating by supervisors.

Income   Beginning salaries average about $19,700 a year. Earnings vary for firefighters with experience depending on city size and region of the country. Average earnings range from $23,200 in the smallest cities to $31,400 in the largest cities and from $21,500 in the South to $29,300 in the West. Firefighters in supervisory positions may earn significantly more.

Most fire departments provide allowances to pay for protective clothing such as helmets, boots, and rubber coats, and many also provide dress uniforms.

Firefighters are usually covered by liberal pension plans that often provide for retirement at half pay at age 50 after 25 years of service or at any age if disabled in the line of duty.

Additional Sources of Information

Information is available from local civil service commission offices or fire departments.

International Association of Fire Chiefs
1329 18th Street, NW
Washington, DC 20036

International Association of Fire Fighters
1750 New York Avenue NW
Washington, DC 20006

Forester

The Job   The forest lands of the United States—whether publicly or privately owned—must be carefully and efficiently managed if they are to survive. It is the work of the professional forester to develop, manage, and protect forest lands and their resources of timber, water, wildlife, forage, and recreation areas. If properly protected and managed, these resources can be utilized repeatedly without being destroyed.

Foresters often specialize in one type of work such as timber management, outdoor recreation, or forest economics. In these capacities, they might plan and supervise the planting and cutting of trees or devote themselves to watershed management, wildlife protection, disease and insect control, fire prevention, or the development and supervision of recreation areas.

About half of all foresters work for the federal government, most of them in the Forest Service of the Department of Agriculture. State and local governments also employ foresters.

Places of Employment and Working Conditions   Foresters are employed in nearly every state, but the largest numbers are employed in the heavily forested areas of the Northwest, Northeast, and South.

Foresters, especially beginners, spend a great deal of time outdoors in all kinds of weather and often at remote locations. During emergencies such as fires and rescue missions, they may work long hours under difficult and dangerous conditions.

Qualifications, Education, and Training   Anyone interested in forestry as a career should be physically hardy, enjoy working outdoors, and be willing to work in remote areas.

A bachelor's degree with a major in forestry is the minimum requirement, but employers prefer to hire applicants with advanced degrees. About 55 colleges and universities offer bachelor's or higher degrees in forestry, most of them accredited by the Society of American Foresters. Scientific and technical forestry subjects, liberal arts, and communication skills are emphasized along with courses in forest economics and business administration. All schools encourage work experience in forestry or conservation, and many of the colleges require at least one summer at a college-operated field camp.

Potential and Advancement   About 29,000 persons are employed as foresters. Employment opportunities are expected to grow slowly due to the government's budget restrictions. The job outlook, however, is better than in the past because of an expected wave in retirements and recent declines in the number of graduates in forestry.

Advancement in this field depends on experience, with federally employed foresters able to advance through supervisory positions to regional forest supervisors or to top administrative positions.

Income   Starting salaries for federally employed foresters vary: those having a bachelor's degree start at $16,973 or $21,023 a year, depending on their

academic achievement; those with a master's degree, $21,023 or $25,717; those with a Ph.D., $31,294; and those with Ph.D.s who work in research, $37,294.

The average salary for foresters employed by the federal government is $38,617 a year.

Salaries in state and local governments are generally lower.

Additional Sources of Information

American Forestry Association
P.O. Box 2000
Washington, DC 20013

Society of American Foresters
5400 Grosvenor Lane
Bethesda, MD 20814

Chief
U.S. Forest Service
U.S. Department of Agriculture
14th Street and Independence Avenue, SW
Washington, DC 20250

Forestry Technician

The Job   Forestry technicians assist foresters in the care and management of forest lands and their resources. They estimate timber production; inspect for insect damage; supervise surveying and road-building crews; work in flood control and water quality programs; supervise firefighting crews; supervise planting and reforestation programs; and maintain forest areas for hunting, camping, and other recreational use.

The federal government employs about half of all forestry technicians. Many technicians employed by the federal and state governments work only during the summer or during the spring and fall fire seasons.

Places of Employment and Working Conditions   Forestry
technicians work throughout the country in just about every state.

Outdoor work in all kinds of weather is the norm for this job field. In emergencies such as forest fires and floods, the working hours are very long, and the work can be dangerous. In many areas, the work is seasonal.

Qualifications, Education, and Training   Good physical condition, stamina, a love of the outdoors, and the ability to work with or without supervision and with a variety of people are all necessary for a forestry technician.

High school should include as many science courses as possible.

Some technicians acquire their training through experience on firefighting crews, in recreation work, or in tree nurseries. Because this is a very competitive job field, however, those with specialized training in forestry have better opportunities for full-time employment.

One- and two-year courses for forestry technicians are available in technical institutes, junior colleges, and colleges and universities. Subjects studied include mathematics, biology and botany, land surveying, tree identification, aerial photography interpretation, and timber harvesting.

Potential and Advancement   This field is expected to grow more slowly than the average for all occupations through the year 2005. The number of applicants will exceed job openings due to the popularity of the work.

Income   Salaries range from $16,000 to $18,300 a year. Experienced forestry technicians may earn over $20,000 a year.

Additional Sources of Information

American Forestry Association
P.O. Box 2000
Washington, DC 20013

Society of American Foresters
5400 Grosvenor Lane
Bethesda, MD 20814

Chief
U.S. Forest Service
U.S. Department of Agriculture
14th Street and Independence Avenue, SW
Washington, DC 20250

Geographer

The Job   Geographers study and analyze the distribution of land forms; climate; soils and vegetation; and mineral, water, and human resources. They also study the distribution of cultural phenomena such as economics, politics, medicine, and transportation. These studies help to explain the patterns of human settlement.

The federal government employs geographers for mapping, intelligence work, and remote sensing interpretation. State and local governments employ geographers on planning and development commissions.

Cartographers design and construct maps and charts. They also conduct research in surveying and mapping procedures. They work with aerial photographs and analyze data from remote sensing equipment on satellites.

Places of Employment and Working Conditions   Geographers are employed throughout the country and on foreign assignment as well. The largest single concentration of geographers is in the Washington, D.C., area.

Fieldwork sometimes entails assignment to remote areas and less developed regions of the world. A geographer should be prepared for the physical and social hardships such relocation may require.

Qualifications, Education, and Training   Anyone interested in this field should enjoy reading, studying, and research and be able to work independently. Good communication skills are also necessary.

High school experience should include as many mathematics and science courses as possible.

A bachelor's degree with a major in geography is the first step for a would-be geographer. Course work should also include some specialty fields such as cartography, aerial photography, or statistical analysis.

Advanced degrees are required for most teaching positions and for advancement in business and government; a Ph.D. is necessary for the top jobs. Mathematics, statistics, and computer science are of increasing importance in graduate studies; students interested in foreign regional geography are usually required to take a foreign language as well.

Potential and Advancement In general, this field will grow, but some areas will offer more job opportunities than others. The federal government will employ a growing number of geographers and cartographers, as will state and local governments. There will be a demand for geographers who specialize in geographic information systems (GIS), which combine computer graphics, artificial intelligence, and high-speed communication to store, retrieve, manipulate, and map geographic data. Persons with only a bachelor's degree will face tough competition for jobs.

Advancement in this field depends on experience and additional education.

Income Geographers with a bachelor's degree and no experience have starting salaries of $17,000 or $21,000 a year with the federal government. Those with a master's degree start at $25,700 and those with a Ph.D., $31,100. Some individuals start at $37,300.

The average salary for geographers employed by the federal government is $46,200 a year.

Additional Sources of Information

Association of American Geographers
1710 16th Street, NW
Washington, DC 20009

Geologist

The Job By examining surface rocks and rock samples drilled from beneath the surface, geologists study the structure, composition, and history of the earth's crust. Their work is important in the search for mineral resources and oil and in the study of predicting earthquakes. Geologists are also employed to advise on the construction of buildings, dams, and highways.

Geologists study plant and animal fossils as well as minerals and rocks. Some specialize in the study of the ocean floor. *Volcanologists* study active and inactive volcanoes and lava flows. *Mineralogists* analyze and classify minerals and precious stones.

Geologists are beginning to play an important role in the study, preservation, and cleaning up of the environment. They design and monitor waste disposal sites, reclaim contaminated water and land, and preserve water supplies. They also help to locate safe sites for hazardous waste facilities, nuclear power plants, and landfills.

The federal government employs over 6,000 geologists in the U.S. Geological Survey, the Bureau of Land Management, the Minerals Management Service, the Bureau of Mines, and the Bureau of Reclamation. Others work for the departments of Defense, Agriculture, Commerce, and Energy and the Environmental Protection Agency. State and local governments employ geologists in highway construction and survey work.

Places of Employment and Working Conditions
Some geologists work primarily in an office, while others spend some of their time in an office or laboratory and the rest of their time at field sites. Geologists often work at remote locations, travelling by helicopter or four-wheel drive vehicle. They may cover many miles on foot. Their research may also take them underground or to offshore oil rigs.

Qualifications, Education, and Training
Curiosity, analytical thinking, and physical stamina are all necessary for a geologist.

High school should include as much science and mathematics as possible.

A bachelor's degree in geology or a related field is the basic preparation and is adequate for some entry-level jobs. A doctorate is becoming more important for employment in some federal agencies.

Over 500 colleges and universities offer bachelor's degrees in geology or geophysics. More than 270 universities offer advanced degrees in geology or geophysics.

Potential and Advancement
This field is expected to grow about as fast as the average for all occupations through the year 2005. Job opportunities will increase as exploration for new sources for oil and gas increases. There will also be opportunities in environmental protection.

Those with advanced degrees will have the most job opportunities and the best chances for promotion.

Income
The federal government pays an average annual salary to geologists in managerial, supervisory, and nonsupervisory positions of $47,669. The average annual salary paid to all geologists employed by the federal government is $52,025.

Additional Sources of Information

American Geological Institute
4220 King Street
Alexandria, VA 22302

Geological Society of America
P.O. Box 9140
3300 Penrose Place
Boulder, CO 80301

Government Chief Executive and Legislator

The Job   The goal of many workers who choose a career in government is to become a chief executive or legislator. While these positions, at the various levels of government, sometimes carry with them enormous power, they also require taking on tremendous responsibilities. Those who are able to achieve these positions must maintain the efficient and effective operation of the government while, at the same time, meeting the needs of the public that has elected them.

Heading up units of government is the responsibility of chief executives. Included among chief executives are the president and vice-president of the United States, state governors and lieutenant governors, and county commissioners, township supervisors, mayors, and city managers. Except for city managers, who are appointed by the city council, all of these officials are elected. (See the entry "City Manager" for specific information on this position.)

The job of a government chief executive is similar to the chief executive officer of a corporation. Those holding this position must take responsibility for the performance of the government over which they preside. They must work with legislators to determine constituents' needs and devise plans and policies for addressing those needs in an effective way. Because they have such a wide variety of duties, chief executives must appoint others to manage government departments and agencies; in this way they can see that policies are being carried out and laws are being enforced.

Chief executives consult with advisors and legislators to compare ideas and determine the best means of addressing constituents' needs. They meet with leaders of other governments to cooperate in solving mutual problems. They are also responsible for providing a budget and seeing that the government's resources are being used appropriately.

Chief executives who preside over larger units of government have many aides and assistants; those who preside over smaller units may do much of this work themselves.

Legislators make and amend existing laws. They include U.S. senators and representatives, state senators and representatives, county legislators, and city and town council members. Legislators must be aware of the needs and problems confronting their constituents and the nation as a whole so that they can propose and pass laws that will effectively resolve them. They accomplish this by doing research; meeting with constituents, experts, consultants, lobbyists, and other legislators; and conferring with the chief executive and heads of departments and agencies.

Legislators at the highest levels of government usually have staff members and aides who assist them in their work.

Places of Employment and Working Conditions
The size of the government unit determines working conditions. While local council members may meet once a month, U.S. Congress members, governors and lieutenant governors, and chief executives of larger government units may work 60 or more hours a week throughout the entire year. State legislators are usually in session for only a few months of the year. During those times, legislators work full time while working part time the rest of the year. Local officials typically work part time.

Because of the great responsibility of their jobs, government chief executives and legislators experience a great deal of pressure and stress in their jobs. They are on call at all hours in case of emergencies. Travel is typically required of those working in higher levels of government.

Qualifications, Education, and Training
There are certain minimum age, residency, and citizenship requirements for most leadership positions in government. But because voters determine whether a candidate is qualified for a leadership position in government, those who want to become a chief executive or legislator must determine how to become elected.

Certain characteristics are important for success as chief executive or legislator. Candidates must be able to make fair decisions. Confidence in themselves and their supporters is important, as is the ability to motivate others. They must be honest and must be able to communicate their ideas effectively in order to gain the support and confidence of their constituents. Good health, energy, stamina, and fund-raising skills are important for running a successful campaign.

Those who are elected to office often have a track record of success in their careers and in public service. They are often business leaders, teachers, or members of the legal profession. They have often served as voluntary leaders of groups that have placed them in the public eye, such as school boards, political campaigns, and charities.

Potential and Advancement

There are 71,000 chief executives and legislators, and five out of six are employed by local governments. There are 535 members of the United States Congress and about 7,500 state legislators. Little change is expected in these numbers through the year 2005.

Newcomers may fill these positions if they are able to defeat incumbents in elections. There is typically stiff competition to fill positions.

Advancement for chief executives and legislators depends on their ability to be re-elected. Those working in lower levels of government often aspire to positions in higher levels. For example, a state senator may gain experience and become well known among constituents and then run for a position in the U.S. Congress. A state governor whose effectiveness becomes well known may run for the U.S. presidency.

Income

Earnings depend on the level of the government for which an individual works and whether he or she works full time the entire year, full time for part of the year, or part time. Salaries range from nothing for a member of a small-town council to $200,000 a year for the U.S. president.

Mayors earn an average annual salary of about $9,400. In cities with a population of 2,500 or fewer, salaries average about $1,900; in cities with a population over a million, over $80,000.

Forty states pay annual salaries to their legislators, which average about $21,000. The other ten states pay per diem while legislatures are in session. The highest amounts are paid by the largest states.

Governors' salaries range from $35,000 in Arkansas to $130,000 in New York. Most governors also receive transportation and housing. Salaries for lieutenant governors average over $47,000 a year.

Additional Sources of Information

Council of State Governments
P.O. Box 11910
Iron Works Pike
Lexington, KY 40578

The National Association of Counties
440 First Street, NW
Washington, DC 20001

Information may also be obtained from your elected representative and the local library.

Home Economist

The Job   The comfort and well-being of families and the products, services, and practices that affect them are the concern of home economists. Some have a broad knowledge of the whole professional field, while others specialize in consumer affairs, housing, home management, home furnishings and equipment, food and nutrition, clothing and textiles, or child development and family relations.

The federal government employs home economists in the U.S. Department of Agriculture to research the buying and spending habits of families in all socioeconomic groups and to develop budget guides for them. Federal, state, and local governments employ home economists in social welfare programs to instruct clients in homemaking skills and family living.

Some home economists work as cooperative extension service agents and provide adult education programs for rural communities and farmers. They also provide youth programs such as 4-H clubs and train and supervise volunteer leaders for these programs.

Most home economists are women, although a growing number of men have entered the field in recent years.

Places of Employment and Working Conditions   A 40-hour workweek is the norm in this field, but those in teaching positions usually work some evening hours.

Qualifications, Education, and Training   Leadership, poise, communication skills, the ability to work with people of many cultures and levels of income, and an interest in family welfare are necessary for this work.

High school courses should include English, home economics, health, mathematics, chemistry, and the social sciences. Part-time or summer jobs in children's camps or day nurseries provide valuable experience.

A bachelor's degree in home economics qualifies graduates for most entry-level positions. A master's degree or Ph.D is required for some research and supervisory positions and extension service specialists.

Potential and Advancement

Job competition for home economists will be stiff through the year 2005. Concern over product quality and environmental issues will bring about a slight increase in job opportunities for home economists who work in research. The best jobs will go to those with advanced degrees or experience.

Research home economists advance by becoming the head of a department or team. They can also become administrators or executives in government agencies.

Income

Home economists who work for the federal government have starting salaries of about $15,000 to $19,000 a year. Those with experience earn annual salaries of about $19,500 to $28,000 or more.

Additional Sources of Information

American Home Economics Association
2010 Massachusetts Avenue, NW
Washington, DC 20036

Internal Revenue Agent

The Job

Internal revenue agents examine and audit the financial records of individuals, businesses, and other organizations to determine their correct federal income tax liability.

In district offices throughout the country, agents audit income tax returns, handle investigations, and provide information and assistance to the public on questions concerning income taxes.

A rapidly expanding career field with the Internal Revenue Service is computerized information processing. Job openings for mathematicians, statisticians, computer programmers, systems analysts, economists, and other computer specialists are increasing steadily.

Places of Employment and Working Conditions   Internal revenue agents work throughout the country as well as in Washington, D.C.

Agents usually work a normal 40-hour week with occasional overtime during peak work loads. Agents involved in auditing and investigative work may spend some time in travel.

Qualifications, Education, and Training   Aptitude for mathematics, the ability to do detailed work accurately and to work independently, patience, tact, and the ability to get along with people are important for this job.

In high school, a college preparatory course with plenty of mathematics should be followed.

A college degree is required for all internal revenue agents. A degree in accounting or law or a liberal arts degree with some study of accounting and directly related subjects has been the traditional background for agents. Degrees in computer-related specialties are now also accepted.

Most new agents are hired by district offices through local college recruitment programs. Applicants must pass a civil service examination before being hired.

Potential and Advancement   Requirements have remained stable in recent years with increases in work load being handled with the aid of computers. The number of interested applicants and the available job openings have been just about equal. The employment outlook is good.

Opportunities for advancement are numerous in the Internal Revenue Service. Agents may be promoted to supervisory and management positions in district and regional offices and to top-level positions in Washington, D.C.

Income   Beginning salaries range from $17,000 to $22,000 a year, depending on education and college grades. Within-grade increases and promotions are rapid, for the most part.

Experienced agents in the Internal Revenue Service earn from $30,000 to $38,000 a year.

Additional Sources of Information

Contact the Internal Revenue Service district office in your locality.

Interpreter

The Job   Oral interpretation is needed whenever a difference in language creates a barrier between people of different cultures.

There are two basic types of interpretation: simultaneous and consecutive. In simultaneous interpretation, the interpreter translates what is being said in one language as the speaker continues to speak in another. This requires both fluency and speed on the part of the interpreter and is made possible by the use of electronic equipment that allows the transmission of simultaneous speeches. Simultaneous interpretation is preferred for conferences and meetings. Conference interpreters often work in a glass-enclosed booth using earphones and a microphone. Those attending the conference can tune into their preferred language by turning a dial or pushing a button.

In consecutive interpretation, the speaker and the interpreter take turns speaking. In addition to having fluency in the language, a consecutive interpreter must also have a good memory and usually will take notes to give a full and accurate translation. This method is very time consuming but is the usual method for person-to-person interpretation.

The U.S. departments of State and Justice are the major employers of full-time interpreters in the federal government. The United Nations (UN) employs full-time interpreters as well.

Free-lance interpreters usually work on short-term contracts, although some assignments can be of longer duration. The greatest number of free-lance interpreters work under contract for the U.S. Department of State, serving as escort interpreters for foreign visitors to the United States.

Places of Employment and Working Conditions   This is a relatively small job field with the largest concentration of interpreters in New York City and Washington, D.C.

The conditions under which interpreters work vary widely. Free-lance interpreters have little job security because of the fluctuations in demand for their service. Free-lance assignments can last from a few days to several weeks. Although interpreters do not necessarily work long hours, they often work irregular hours, with escort interpreters often required to do a great deal of traveling.

Qualifications, Education, and Training
Anyone interested in becoming an interpreter should be an articulate speaker and have good hearing. This work requires quickness, accuracy, tact, and emotional stamina to deal with the tensions of the job. Interpreters must be dependable as to the honesty of their interpretations and have a sense of responsibility as to the confidentiality of their work.

A complete command of two languages or more is the usual requirement for an interpreter. Interpreters at the UN must know at least three of the six official UN languages: Arabic, Chinese, English, French, Russian, and Spanish.

An extensive and up-to-date working vocabulary and ease in making the transition from one language structure to another are necessary as well as the ability to instantly call to mind appropriate words or idioms of the language.

Many individuals may qualify on the basis of their own foreign backgrounds, and the experience of living abroad is also very important. Interpreters should be generally well informed.

Although there is no standard requirement for entry into this profession, a university education generally is essential. In the United States, two schools offer special programs for interpreters. Foreign language proficiency is an entry requirement for both.

Applicants to Georgetown University School of Languages and Linguistics in Washington, D.C., must qualify on the basis of an entrance examination and previous studies at the university level; they usually hold a bachelor's degree and often a master s degree. The school awards a certificate of proficiency as a conference interpreter upon successful completion of a one- or two-year course of study.

The Department of Translation and Interpretation at the Monterey Institute of Foreign Studies in Monterey, California, offers a two-year graduate program leading to a master's degree in intercultural communication and a graduate certificate in translation, translation/interpretation, or conference interpretation. School entrance requirements include a bachelor's degree, an aptitude test, fluency in English plus one other language if studying translation, or two other languages for the interpretation field. After two semesters of basic courses in translating and interpreting, applicants must pass a qualifying examination for entrance into the translation or interpretation programs.

Potential and Advancement
There are about 1,000 interpreters working full-time in the United States.

Only highly qualified applicants will find jobs in this field. There is stiff competition for the very limited number of job openings, and the number of openings is not expected to increase through the year 2000. Some openings will occur, however, to replace those who retire or leave the field for other reasons. In the past, any increase in the demand for full-time interpreters has been slight and usually temporary and has been met by the existing pool of free-lance interpreters.

Income   Beginning salaries for full-time interpreters are around $20,000 a year. Experienced interpreters earn annual salaries ranging from about $30,000 to $35,000 a year. Some high-level interpreters working for the federal government earn $60,000 and up a year.

Additional Sources of Information

The American Association of Language Specialists
1000 Connecticut Avenue, NW
Suite 9
Washington, DC 20036

Department of Translation and Interpretation
Monterey Institute of Foreign Studies
P.O. Box 1978
Monterey, CA 93940

Division of Interpretation and Translation
School of Languages and Linguistics
Georgetown University
Washington, DC 20057

Language Services Division
U.S. Department of State
Washington, DC 20520

Judge

The Job   Laws are the rules of conduct established by the government that enable the members of society to resolve conflicts peaceably and justly. It is the job of judges to ensure that when conflicts arise, federal, state, or local laws are applied appropriately in settling a civil dispute or determining guilt and punishment in a criminal case. Judges preside over many different types of cases, from simple traffic offenses to disputes over contracts to child custody disagreements. They must make sure that in a trial the hearings are conducted in a manner that protects the legal rights of all the parties that are involved. They listen to attorneys argue the cases of their clients and make sure that the rules and procedures regarding evidence and testimony are followed.

Sometimes judges hold pretrial hearings, during which they determine whether there is enough evidence to warrant a trial or whether a person charged with a crime should be held in jail or may be released during the trial.

In jury trials, juries decide the outcome of cases, but judges must decide cases when the law does not require a jury or the accused party waives his or her right to a jury. In a jury trial, the judge instructs the jury regarding the laws that apply to a case and reminds them that their decision must be based on facts derived from the evidence presented during the trial. In criminal cases in many states, judges must then determine sentences for those who are declared guilty. In civil cases, judges often determine the amount of the damages awarded.

The responsibilities of a judge vary according to his or her jurisdiction. In federal and state court systems, general trial court judges have jurisdiction over any case. Appellate court judges have the authority to overrule decisions made by trial courts or administrative law judges if some error in the procedure of a case is found or if legal precedent does not support the decision of a lower court.

Most state court judges are limited by law to preside over certain types of cases such as traffic violations, misdemeanors, and pretrial hearings.

Administrative law judges work for government agencies and rule on appeals of agency administrative decisions, such as whether a person is eligible for worker's compensation, protection of the environment, or compliance with economic regulatory requirements.

Places of Employment and Working Conditions   Judges are employed throughout the country. They do most of their work in courtrooms, their own offices, and law libraries.

Some judges work a 40-hour week, but others have very large caseloads that may require over 50 hours a week. Besides the time spent in the courtroom, judges spend many hours preparing for trials, researching, and preparing decisions.

Qualifications, Education, and Training   Judges must be very responsible, have an interest in people and ideas, must have good reasoning and decision-making ability, and must be very honest.

For most judgeships, experience in the practice of law is required or at least strongly preferred. (See the entry "Lawyer" for educational requirements.) Federal judges and state trial and appellate court judges are required to be lawyers or "learned in law." Judges with limited jurisdictions may not be required to be lawyers, but in most states, these positions are being eliminated or those who are not lawyers are being phased out.

Federal administrative judges must be lawyers and pass an exam given by the U.S. Office of Personnel Management. Many state administrative judges are not required to be lawyers, but those with law degrees are preferred.

Judges achieve their positions in different ways and serve different lengths of time. For example, federal judges are appointed by the president with the consent of Congress and serve for life. State judges, on the other hand, are elected and serve for fixed terms, from four to six years.

Potential and Advancement   Employment of judges is expected to increase about as fast as the average for all occupations through the year 2005. There will be intense competition for any openings on the bench.

Income   Federal trial court judges earn an annual salary of $125,100; appellate court judges, $132,700; federal judges with limited jurisdiction, $115,100; and federal administrative law judges, $72,300.

State trial court judges earn average annual salaries of $77,500; and state appellate court judges, $85,300. Salaries for state judges with limited jurisdictions vary widely, from part-time judges who earn $500 a year to full-time judges who earn as much as $98,000.

Additional Sources of Information

Information Services
American Bar Association
750 North Lake Shore Drive
Chicago, IL 60611

Lawyer

The Job   The basic work of lawyers, also called attorneys, involves interpreting the law and applying it to the needs of a particular case or client. Sometimes their job requires them to act as an advocate, representing a client in a criminal or civil case and presenting arguments to support his or her case. Sometimes lawyers provide legal advice regarding personal or business matters. In preparation for their work, lawyers must research relevant laws and judicial decisions in order to serve the best interests of their clients.

There are many different fields that lawyers may specialize in. Some specialize in trial law, representing their clients in the courtroom. These lawyers must be able to speak clearly and assertively and must be able to think quickly. They spend a great deal of time outside of the courtroom researching, interviewing clients and witnesses, and preparing for trial.

Still others specialize in corporate law, often working for a company and offering advice regarding its business activities. Other specialties include international law, communications law, patent law, tax law, real estate law, or labor law.

A large group of lawyers works for the government. They may work in criminal law as an employee of a state attorney general, a prosecutor, a public defender, or a court. They also work for federal government agencies, such as the departments of Justice and the Treasury and for regulatory agencies such as the Securities and Exchange Commission and the Equal Employment Opportunities Commission.

Most lawyers work in private practice, either alone or in a law firm. They may handle a variety of legal matters—making wills, settling estates, preparing property deeds, and drawing up contracts.

Places of Employment and Working Conditions   Lawyers
are needed in every community and by businesses and government agencies throughout the country.

Lawyers often work long hours and are under considerable pressure when a case is being tried. Those in private practice, however, can determine their own hours and caseloads and are usually able to work past the usual retirement age.

Qualifications, Education, and Training   Assertiveness, an interest in people and ideas, the ability to inspire trust and confidence, and top-notch debating and writing skills are necessary for this field. A successful

lawyer must be able to research and analyze a case and to think conceptually and logically.

High school courses that develop language and verbal skills are important. Typing, American history, civics and government, and any training in debating, public speaking, or acting will prove useful.

At least seven years of full-time study beyond high school are necessary to obtain a law degree. This study includes four years of college and three years of law school. Students attending law school on a part-time basis may take four years or longer to complete the work.

Although there is no specific prelaw college program, the best undergraduate training is one that gives the student a broad educational background while developing the writing, speaking, and thinking skills necessary for a legal career. Majors in the social sciences, natural sciences, and humanities are suitable and should include courses in economics, philosophy, logic, history, and government. Good grades are very important.

Most law schools test an applicant's aptitude for the study of law by requiring the applicant to take the Law School Admission Test (LSAT). Competition for admission to law school is intense. At one point in the mid-1970s, the ratio of applicants to available openings was ten to one. Although this has slowed to some extent, stiff competition for entrance into law school will remain for the foreseeable future, particularly for the more prestigious law schools.

Students should attend a law school that is approved by the American Bar Association (ABA) or by an individual state. ABA approval indicates that the school meets the minimum standards of education necessary for practice in any state; state-approved schools that lack ABA approval prepare graduates for practice in that particular state only. A few states recognize the study of law done entirely in a law office or a combination of law office and law school study. California will accept the study of law by correspondence course, if all other qualifications are met. Several states require the registration and approval of law students by the state board of examiners before they enter law school or during the early years of legal study.

The first part of law school is devoted to the study of fundamental courses such as constitutional law, contracts, property law, and judicial procedure. Specialized courses in such fields as tax, labor, or corporate law are also offered. The second part of law school consists of practical training through participation in school-sponsored legal aid activities, courtroom practice in the school's practice court under the supervision of experienced lawyers, and through writing on legal issues for the school's law journal.

Upon successful completion of law school, graduates usually receive the degree of doctor of laws (J.D.) or bachelor of laws (L.L.B.). Those who intend to teach, do research, or specialize usually continue with advanced study.

All states require a lawyer to be admitted to the state bar before practicing law. Requirements include a written examination, at least three years of college, and graduation from an ABA- or state-approved law school.

Potential and Advancement Although this field is expected to grow steadily, a rapid increase in the number of law school graduates in recent years has created keen competition for available jobs. This situation will probably continue. Graduates of prestigious law schools and those who rank high in their graduating class will have the best chance of securing salaried positions with law firms, corporations, and government agencies, and as law clerks (research assistants) for judges. Lawyers who wish to establish a new practice will find the best opportunities in small towns and in expanding suburban areas.

Lawyers advance from positions as law clerks to experienced lawyers through progressively more responsible work. Many establish their own practice. After years of experience, some lawyers become judges.

Income Beginning lawyers working in private industry earn, on average, about $47,000 a year; graduates of prestigious law schools in some cases start at over $80,000. Starting salaries in the federal government are about $25,000 or $31,000 a year, depending on academic record and personal qualifications.

Salaries for experienced lawyers vary greatly depending on the type, size, and location of employer. The average annual salary for the most experienced lawyers is over $120,000, but some senior partners in top law firms earn over a million dollars annually. General attorneys working for the federal government earn an average of $53,300 a year.

Additional Sources of Information

Association of American Law Schools
1201 Connecticut Avenue, NW
Suite 800
Washington, DC 20036

Information Services
American Bar Association
750 North Lake Shore Drive
Chicago, IL 60611

Mechanical Engineer

The Job   The production, transmission, and use of power is the concern of mechanical engineers. They design and develop power-producing machines such as internal combustion engines and power-using machines such as air-conditioning systems, machine tools, and robots.

This is the broadest engineering discipline, and the work of mechanical engineers varies greatly because of the wide array of possible applications of their skills and training. They may work with engines powering a ship or an air-conditioning system for an office building.

Almost every federal government agency employs a few mechanical engineers, but most work for the armed forces.

Places of Employment and Working Conditions   Mechanical engineers work in all parts of the country.

Many engineers work in laboratories or at construction sites while others work in an office all the time. A few engineers are required to travel extensively. Many engineers work 40 hours a week, but deadlines may bring extra pressure to a job.

Qualifications, Education, and Training   The ability to think analytically, a capacity for detail, and the ability to work as part of a team are all necessary. Good communication skills are important.

Mathematics and the sciences must be emphasized in high school.

A bachelor's degree in engineering is the minimum requirement in this field. In a typical curriculum, the first two years are spent in the study of basic sciences such as physics and chemistry and mathematics, introductory engineering, and some liberal arts courses. The remaining years are usually devoted to specialized engineering courses. Engineering programs can last from four to six years. Those requiring five or six years to complete may award a master's degree or may provide a cooperative plan of study plus practical work experience with a nearby industry.

Because of rapid changes in technology, many engineers continue their education throughout their careers. A graduate degree is necessary for most teaching and research positions and for many management jobs. Some persons obtain graduate degrees in business administration.

Engineering graduates usually work under the supervision of an experienced engineer or in a company training program until they become acquainted with the requirements of a particular company or industry.

All states require licensing of engineers whose work may affect life, health, or property or who offer their services to the public. Those who are licensed, about one-third of all engineers, are called registered engineers. Requirements include graduation from an accredited engineering school, four years of experience, and a written examination.

Potential and Advancement
Employment of mechanical engineers is expected to grow about as fast as the average for all occupations through the year 2005. However, because many jobs are in the armed forces, cuts in defense spending could result in fewer jobs.

Income
The average annual salary for engineers employed by the federal government is about $49,367.

Additional Sources of Information

Accreditation Board for Engineering and Technology
345 East 47th Street
New York, NY 10017

American Society for Engineering Education
11 Dupont Circle
Suite 200
Washington, DC 20036

The American Society of Mechanical Engineers
34 East 47th Street
New York, NY 10017

Junior Engineering Technical Society (JETS)
1420 King Street
Alexandria, VA 22314

National Society of Professional Engineers
1420 King Street
Alexandria, VA 22314

Society of Women Engineers
345 East 47th Street
Room 305
New York, NY 10017

Meteorologist

The Job   The study of the atmosphere—its physical characteristics, motions, and processes—is the work of meteorologists. Although the best known application of this study is in weather forecasting, meteorologists are also engaged in research and problem solving in the fields of air pollution, transportation, agriculture, and industrial operations.

Physical meteorologists study the chemical and electrical properties of the atmosphere as they affect the formation of clouds, rain, and snow. *Climatologists* analyze past data on wind, rainfall, and temperature to determine weather patterns for a given area; this work is important in designing buildings and in planning effective land use. *Operational* or *synoptic meteorologists* study current weather information, such as temperature, humidity, air pressure, and wind velocity, in order to make short- and long-range forecasts.

The largest single employer of civilian meteorologists is the National Oceanic and Atmospheric Administration (NOAA), which employs about 1,800 meteorologists, most of whom work for the National Weather Service at stations in all parts of the United States. The Department of Defense employs nearly 300 civilian meteorologists.

Places of Employment and Working Conditions   Meteorologists work in all areas of the United States, in or near cities as well as in remote areas.

Since they continue around the clock, seven days a week, jobs in weather stations involve night and weekend shifts. In large offices, meteorologists work in teams, while in small offices at remote locations, they often work alone.

Qualifications, Education, and Training   Curiosity, analytical thinking, and attention to detail are necessary qualities for a meteorologist.

High school experience should include as many science and mathematics courses as possible.

For entry-level meteorologists, the federal government requires a bachelor's degree, but not necessarily in meteorology. However, it does require that beginning meteorologists have completed the following course work: 20 hours of meteorology courses, including 6 hours in weather analysis and forecasting and 6 hours in dynamic meteorology; 6 hours of differential and integral calculus; 6 hours of calculus-based physics; 3 hours of computer science; and 6 hours of course work relevant to a physical science major, such as statistics, chemistry, physical oceanography, or physical climatology.

Potential and Advancement

Job opportunities for meteorologists should be more plentiful in the next five to ten years than they have been in the past. The National Weather Service plans to increase its employment of meteorologists in order to improve both its short- and long-term forecasting. Employment of meteorologists in branches of the federal government other than the National Weather Service is not expected to increase.

Meteorologists with advanced degrees and experience can advance to supervisory and administrative positions.

Income

The federal government pays an average starting salary of $16,973 or $21,023 a year, depending on college grades, to meteorologists with a bachelor's degree; $21,023 or $25,717 to those with a master's degree; and $31,116 or $37,294 to those with a Ph.D.

The average annual salary for experienced meteorologists employed by the federal government is $44,706.

Additional Sources of Information

American Meteorological Society
45 Beacon Street
Boston, MA 02108

Officer, U.S. Armed Forces

The Job   The purpose of the U.S. armed forces is to deter aggression and defend the country in times of war. Branches of the armed forces include the Army, which provides land-based defense; the Air Force, which protects air and space; the Navy, which prepares for sea defense; the Marine Corps, part of the Department of the Navy, which offers land support for naval operations; and the Coast Guard, under the Department of Transportation except in times of war, which sees that maritime laws are enforced, rescues distressed vessels and aircraft at sea, prevents smuggling, and operates aids to navigation.

The armed forces, America's largest employer, offers educational and work experiences in thousands of occupations; there are more than 1,600 advanced military occupational specialties for officers. Occupational groups include the following: infantry, gun crews, and seamanship specialties; electronic equipment repair occupations; communications and intelligence specialties; medical and dental occupations; technical and allied specialty occupations; functional support and administrative occupations; electrical and mechanical equipment repair occupations; craft occupations; and service and supply occupations.

A career as an officer in the Army, Navy, Marines, or Coast Guard may be achieved through different methods: the Reserve Officers Training Corps (ROTC), the service academies, Officer Candidate School (OCS), the National Guard State Officer Candidate School, the Uniformed Services University of Health Sciences, and other programs.

Women are eligible to enter almost 90 percent of all military specialties.

Places of Employment and Working Conditions   Members of the U.S. armed forces serve throughout the world. Although some effort is made to allow choice of location at the time of enlistment, assignments are not always to the location of choice.

Military personnel must be disciplined in every aspect of their lives—protocol governs everything from the manner in which they dress to the people with whom they may socialize. Depending on the branch of the service to which an officer belongs, travel may be required, particularly for those assigned to ships or overseas assignments.

During times of war, those who are in combat face danger. Training activities may be dangerous as well.

Officers who receive their training at one of the service academies as well as officers who receive their training and college education through ROTC scholarships are obligated to serve on active duty for a stipulated period of time. Other officers serve various lengths of time on active duty.

Qualifications, Education, and Training
Leadership qualities are important for anyone interested in a career as an officer. Applicants must be between 18 and 28 years of age (there are a few exceptions), U.S. citizens, and in good physical condition. The service academies require a rigorous physical examination and have specific height, weight, eyesight, color vision, and hearing requirements.

High school courses should include English, science, and mathematics. Extracurricular activities that develop leadership qualities are valuable.

Ninety percent of the officers in the armed forces are college graduates, and it is very difficult to achieve this status without some college education.

ROTC programs are offered at colleges and universities. Along with their regular course work, trainees take two to five hours of military training. After graduation, they serve as officers on active duty for an established period of time. During the last two years of their ROTC program, students receive a monthly allowance and additional pay for summer training. Scholarships are available on a competitive basis.

College graduates can become officers in the armed forces through OCS programs. Applications should be made at local recruiting offices. OCS training lasts from 9 to 39 weeks, depending on branch of service and previous military training.

Applicants for West Point, Annapolis, and the Air Force Academy must be nominated by their congressional representative. The Coast Guard Academy does not require candidates to be appointed; it recruits through an annual national competition. The Army, Navy, and Air Force academies require the College Board Entrance Exam, while the Coast Guard requires the Scholastic Aptitude Test (SAT) or the American College Testing Assessment (ACT). High school guidance counselors can usually provide up-to-date information on requirements at the service academies, or interested students may write to the academies directly.

Those with training in certain medical professions may be directly appointed as officers. The military does provide financial assistance for training in the health professions in return for specified periods of service. Medical students may apply to the Uniformed Services University of Health Sciences and receive free tuition in a program leading to an M.D. degree. In return, they must serve for seven years in the military or the Public Health Service.

Potential and Advancement
Job opportunities should be good in the military through the year 2005 in spite of the cutbacks in personnel that have resulted from the reduced threat from the Soviet Union and other Warsaw Pact

countries. About 15,000 new officers must be recruited each year to replace those who complete their enlistment or retire.

There are different criteria for promotion in each of the branches of the armed services. Promotion is usually based on such factors as length of service and grade, job performance, a supervisor's recommendation, and written examinations.

Income   Depending on their pay grade level, officers with less than two years of experience earn monthly salaries ranging between $1,445 and $2,053. They also receive free room and board (or a housing and subsistence allowance), medical and dental benefits, 30 days' paid vacation a year, a military clothing allowance, military supermarket and department store shopping privileges, and travel opportunities. They may receive retirement benefits after 20 years of service.

Additional Sources of Information

Department of the Army
HQUS Army Recruiting Command
Fort Sheridan, IL 60037

USAF Recruiting Service
Directorate of Advertising and Publicity
Randolph Air Force Base, TX 78150

Commandant of the Marine Corps
Headquarters
Washington, DC 20380-0001

Navy Recruiting Command
4015 Wilson Boulevard
Arlington, VA 22203-1991

Commandant
(G-PRJ)
U.S. Coast Guard
Washington, DC 20590

Parole Officer

The Job   An offender who has completed a sentence in prison or jail is usually assigned a parole officer upon release. The ex-offender is required to report to the parole officer at specific time intervals, and the parole officer, in turn, provides counseling and assistance during the transition from prison to community life.

The parole officer helps the ex-offender find a job or secure job training; arranges for welfare or public assistance for the family, if necessary; and provides positive support and a helping hand in any way possible to aid the parolee in his or her return to society. The parole officer's main concern is helping the parolee go straight instead of returning to a life of crime.

Probation officers deal with juvenile delinquents and first offenders who are often released by the court, subject to proper supervision, instead of being sentenced to jail or prison. A probation officer may also be involved in the presentencing investigation of a defendant's family, background, education, and any problems contributing to the defendant's offense.

Parole and probation officers are usually employed by state or municipal governments. In the course of their work, they deal with teachers, chaplains, social workers, rehabilitation counselors, local employers, and community organizations. A number of parole and probation officers come from the ranks of police officers.

Perhaps the most important ingredient in the work of a probation officer is the rapport the officer is able to establish with the juvenile offender. The opportunity to discuss problems with an understanding adult can result in the juvenile's being put on the right track. At the same time, the probation officer must be objective enough not to be deceived by lies or false promises of better behavior.

Places of Employment and Working Conditions   Emotional wear and tear is a factor in the work of parole and probation officers. The frustration of seeing a parolee or a juvenile return to a life of crime in spite of great effort is part of every officer's experience.

In many jobs, the case load itself can be a hindrance to effective work. Instead of carrying the recommended 30 to 50 cases, many parole and probation officers must keep track of up to 100 assigned cases. This makes it virtually impossible to give each person the attention and help that is usually necessary.

Qualifications, Education, and Training
Personal characteristics of understanding, objectivity, good judgment, and patience are necessary. Good communication skills and the ability to motivate people are very important.

High school should include the social sciences, English, and history.

People who work in this field need a bachelor's degree in sociology, psychology, criminology, or law. Those who start out as police officers usually acquire additional training in these fields through college courses. Many employers also require one or two years of experience in a correctional institution or other social agency or a master's degree in sociology or psychology.

Potential and Advancement
Worker shortages in all areas of law enforcement will increase even more as the population grows. The demand for qualified parole and probation officers will be especially great in large metropolitan areas.

Parole and probation officers are not usually promoted to other positions, but they do advance in salary as they gain experience. Some officers advance by acquiring additional education that qualifies them for positions in other areas of law enforcement.

Income
Probation and parole officers earn between $23,000 and $36,000 a year.

Additional Sources of Information

American Correctional Association
4321 Hartwick Road
College Park, MD 20740

National Council on Crime and Delinquency
77 Maiden Lane
San Francisco, CA 94108

Police Officer, Municipal

The Job   The duties of a police officer may include law enforcement, crowd and traffic control, criminal investigations, communications, and specialties such as handwriting and fingerprint identification or chemical and microscopic analysis. All police officers are trained in first aid.

In a small community, police officers perform a wide variety of duties, while in a large city they may be assigned to one type, such as patrol, traffic, canine patrol, accident prevention, or mounted and motorcycle patrols. Law enforcement is complex, and each police force is tailored to meet the particular problems of its own community. A city of any size that has heavy traffic congestion will need more police assigned to accident prevention and traffic control; a city with a high juvenile crime rate will use more officers in criminal investigation and youth aid services.

New police officers usually begin a patrol duty with an experienced officer to become thoroughly familiar with the city and its law enforcement requirements. This probationary period can last from a few months to three years in some communities.

All police officers report to police headquarters at regular intervals by radio or telephone or through police call boxes. They also prepare written reports about their activities and may be called upon to testify in court on cases they handle.

Detectives are plain-clothes police officers whose primary duty is to carry out investigative procedures. They are often assigned to a specific case, such as a murder investigation, or a particular type of case, such as illegal drugs. Detectives gather information and evidence to be used by police and prosecuting attorneys.

Places of Employment and Working Conditions   Police officers work throughout the country in communities of all sizes.

The usual workweek of a police officer is 40 hours, including shift work and weekend and evening hours. Payment for extra hours worked on some police forces takes the form of extra time off. Officers must often work outdoors in all kinds of weather and are subject to call at any time.

Police officers face the constant threat of injury or death in their work. The injury rate for police officers is higher than in many other occupations.

Qualifications, Education, and Training   A police officer should be honest, have a sense of responsibility and good judgment, and enjoy working with people and serving the public. Good health and physical stamina are also necessary.

High school courses should include English, U.S. history, and civics and government. Physical education and sports are very helpful in developing stamina and agility.

Local civil service regulations govern the appointment of police officers in most communities. Candidates must be at least 21 years old, U.S. citizens, meet certain height and weight standards, and pass a rigorous physical examination. Character traits and backgrounds are investigated, and a personality test is sometimes administered. Applicants are usually interviewed by a senior police officer and, in some police departments, by a psychiatrist or psychologist.

An applicant's eligibility for appointment depends upon his or her performance on a competitive examination. Applicants are listed according to their scores on the examination, and when a police department appoints new police officers, it hires the required number of recruits from the top of the list.

Most police departments require a high school education; a few cities require some college training. More and more police departments are encouraging their officers to continue their education and to study subjects such as sociology, psychology, law enforcement, criminal justice, and foreign languages. These courses are available in junior and community colleges as well as four-year colleges and universities.

New police officers go through a training period. In small communities, this may consist of working with experienced officers. Large cities have more formal training programs that last from several weeks to a few months. Officers receive classroom instruction in constitutional law and civil rights, state and local ordinances, accident investigation, patrol, and traffic control. They learn to use a gun, defend themselves from attack, administer first aid, and deal with emergencies.

Experienced police officers improve their performance, keep up-to-date, and prepare for advancement by taking various training courses given at police department academies and colleges. They study crowd-control techniques, civil defense, the latest legal developments that affect police work, and advances in law enforcement equipment.

In some large cities, high school graduates who are still in their teens may be hired as police cadets or trainees. They function as paid civilian employees and do clerical work while they attend training classes. If they have all the necessary qualifications, they may be appointed to the police force at age 21.

Potential and Advancement
Employment of police officers is expected to grow about as fast as the average for all occupations through the year 2005. All police departments are funded by local governments and, since police protection is considered essential, law enforcement expenses usually have a high priority in municipal budgets. As the population grows, the demand for police officers will also grow. Applicants with some college training in law enforcement will have the best job opportunities.

Advancement in police work depends on length of service, job performance, and written examinations. In some large departments, promotion may also allow a police officer to specialize in one type of police work, such as communications, traffic control, or working with juveniles.

Income   Entry-level salaries are about $22,400 a year. Police officers receive periodic increases until they reach the maximum pay rate for their rank. Average maximum is about $28,700.

Higher rank brings a higher salary and periodic increases until maximum. The average salary for sergeants ranges from $18,900 in small communities to $37,300 in larger cities. For police chiefs, average salaries range from $22,000 in small communities to over $90,000 in larger cities.

Police officers are usually covered by liberal plans that allow them to retire after 20 or 25 years of service at half pay. Most police departments furnish revolvers, nightsticks, handcuffs, and other equipment and provide an allowance for uniforms.

Additional Sources of Information
Information is available from local police departments and civil service commissions.

Police Officer, State

The Job   State police officers, sometimes called state troopers, patrol the highways throughout the United States. They enforce traffic laws, issue traffic tickets to motorists who violate those laws, provide information to travelers, handle traffic control and summon emergency equipment to the scene of an accident or other emergency, sometimes check the weight of commercial vehicles, and conduct driver examinations.

In several areas that do not have a local police force, state police officers may investigate crime. They also help city and county police forces to catch lawbreakers and control civil disturbances.

Some officers are assigned to training assignments in state police schools or to investigate specializations such as fingerprint classification or chemical and microscopic analysis of criminal evidence. A few have administrative duties.

Places of Employment and Working Conditions   State police officers often work irregular hours since police protection is provided 24 hours a day. Sometimes they must work weekends and holidays.

State police officers spend most of their time driving in all kinds of weather. They may be involved in dangerous situations and have to risk their lives in the line of duty.

Qualifications, Education, and Training   Honesty, a sense of responsibility, and a desire to serve the public are important. Physical strength and agility are necessary, and height, weight, and eyesight standards must be met.

High school courses in English, government or civics, U.S. history, and physics are helpful. Physical education and sports develop stamina and agility. Driver education courses or military police training is also valuable.

State civil service regulations govern the appointment of state police officers. Applicants must be U.S. citizens at least 21 years old and must usually have a high school education. Applicants must pass a competitive written examination, a rigorous physical examination, and a character and background investigation.

Recruits enter a formal training program that lasts for several months. They study state laws and jurisdictions, patrol, traffic control, and accident investigation. They learn to use firearms, defend themselves from attack, handle an automobile at high speeds, and give first aid.

State police recruits serve a probationary period ranging from six months to three years. After gaining some experience, some officers take advanced training in police science, administration, law enforcement, criminology, or psychology. Courses in these subjects are offered by junior colleges, four-year colleges and universities, and special police training institutions including the National Academy of the Federal Bureau of Investigation.

Some states hire high school graduates who are still in their teens to serve as cadets. They study police work and perform nonenforcement duties such as clerical work. If they qualify, they may be appointed to the state police force when they reach 21.

Potential and Advancement   Employment of state police officers is expected to grow about as fast as the average for all occupations through the year 2000. Job opportunities should be good, although certain routine police duties are being increasingly handled by civilian firms.

Promotion depends on the amount of time spent in a rank and the individual's standing on competitive examinations.

Income   Beginning officers average about $20,600 a year. Salaries for experienced officers average about $28,700 a year.

Additional Sources of Information
State civil service commissions or state police headquarters, usually located in each state capital, can provide information to anyone interested in a career as a state police officer.

Postal Clerk and Mail Carrier

The Job   Other than the Department of Defense, the U.S. Postal Service is the largest employer of government workers. It employs about 835,000 workers; about 90 percent of those workers are either postal clerks or mail carriers.

Before the carriers can deliver the mail, it must be processed by postal clerks. *Mail handlers* unload the mail as it arrives at a processing center. They separate the mail according to type, such as letters, magazines, and newspapers, and then take the mail to the appropriate sorting and processing area.

After the stamps on the mail have been canceled, the mail is handled by *distribution clerks*, who sort the mail according to destination. These clerks operate letter-sorting machines that sort the letters according to zip code and drop them into the proper slots. Some distribution clerks sort magazines, newspapers, and odd-shaped mail by hand. After this, the mail is sent to the appropriate local post office, where it is sorted according to delivery route.

Postal clerks work in local post offices and sort local mail. They also sell stamps and money orders, weigh packages and collect postage, and answer any questions or complaints that customers may have.

Mail carriers then arrange the mail for delivery on their routes. Carriers may deliver on foot, by vehicle, or a combination of both. They deliver the mail to houses, roadside mailboxes, and office and apartment buildings. They also collect money for postage due and C.O.D. transactions and pick up mail from people on their routes. After they have finished their delivery, carriers return to the post office and take care of minor duties such as readdressing mail that is to be forwarded and turning in any money they have collected.

Places of Employment and Working Conditions   Postal service workers are employed throughout the country in 30,000 post offices and other postal facilities and 485 mail distribution centers.

71

Working conditions vary according to job and place of employment. Postal clerks usually work in clean buildings with good ventilation and lighting. Work may be more physically demanding in small post offices than in large ones, where automated equipment does much of the lifting and moving of the mail.

While postal clerks have a great variety of job duties, mail handlers and distribution clerks may become bored with the routine of their jobs. They also may be required to work nights or weekends, because in large post offices, mail is processed around the clock.

Mail carriers, to a certain extent, are free to set their own schedules. Most start very early in the morning and are finished for the day by the early afternoon. They spend a great deal of time outdoors in all types of weather. They must also lift and sometimes carry heavy sacks of mail.

Qualifications, Education, and Training
Postal workers must have good memories, good coordination, and the ability to read rapidly and accurately. Postal clerks and mail carriers must be courteous and enjoy dealing with the public.

Postal clerks and mail carriers must be at least 16 years old if they are high school graduates and 18 if they are not. Usually, few people are hired before the age of 25 because of the keen competition for jobs and because of a waiting period of one to two years after passing the postal service exam. Workers must also be U.S. citizens or have been granted permanent resident alien status.

Applicants must pass a four-part written test and a physical exam, which includes lifting a mail sack weighing up to 70 pounds. Mail carriers must also have a driver's license, a good driving record, and a passing grade on a road test.

Postal workers are trained on the job by experienced workers. Many post offices offer classroom instruction, and workers are given additional instruction when new procedures or equipment are introduced.

Potential and Advancement
There will be a great deal of competition for jobs with the postal service and far more applicants than openings. The demand for postal clerks will decrease because of the growing use of automation. Opportunities for mail carriers will be a little better because of the continued growth in the volume of mail.

Many postal workers begin as part-time workers and advance by becoming full-time workers as they gain seniority and vacancies occur. Clerks may advance by getting a better assignment such as a day-shift job or a position as a window clerk. Carriers may be able to obtain preferred routes as they gain seniority. Clerks and carriers may advance by becoming supervisors.

Income   Base pay for beginning full-time carriers and postal clerks is $23,640 a year, which reaches a maximum of $29,440 after 10½ years of service. Those working between 6 P.M. and 6 A.M. are paid a supplement.

Earnings for rural delivery carriers are based on the amount of work required to service their routes. They also receive a maintenance allowance when they are required to use their own vehicles.

Postal workers enjoy benefits such as health and life insurance, vacation and sick leave, and a pension plan. Some workers are also paid a uniform allowance.

Additional Sources of Information

Headquarter Personnel Division
U.S. Postal Service
475 L'Enfant Plaza, SW
Washington, DC 20260

Local post offices can also provide information regarding entrance examinations and employment opportunities.

Range Manager

The Job   Range managers are specialists in grazing management. They plan the optimum combination of animals, size of herds, and conservation of vegetation and soil for maximum production without destroying the ecology of an area. Their work also involves timber production, outdoor recreation, erosion control, and fire prevention.

Most range managers work for the federal government in the Forest Service, Soil Conservation Service, and the Bureau of Land Management. State governments employ range managers in fish and game agencies, land agencies, and extension services.

Places of Employment and Working Conditions   Most
range managers work in the West and Alaska.

Outdoor work is usual for range managers, and locations are often remote. They sometimes spend long periods away from home.

Qualifications, Education, and Training   Good physical condition, love of the outdoors, and scientific interest are necessary. Communication skills are also important.

High school should include as many science courses as possible.

Thirty-five colleges and universities offer degree programs in range management or range science; others offer some course work in this field. Courses should include biology; chemistry; physics; mathematics; plant, animal, and soil sciences; and ecology. Electives in economics, computer science, forestry, wildlife, and recreation are desirable.

Graduate degrees in range management are usually necessary for teaching and research positions.

Potential and Advancement   Employment in this field is expected to be slower than the average for all occupations through the year 2005. However, there is an expected wave of retirements among range managers employed by the federal government, and there will be fewer graduates in this field, so there will be more plentiful opportunities than in the past. There will be slow growth in this field due to government budget cuts.

Income   The federal government offers starting salaries of $16,973 or $21,023 a year to beginners with a bachelor's degree. Those with a master's degree started at $21,023 or $25,717, and those with a Ph.D., $31,116. Those with a Ph.D. working in research earn starting salaries of $37,294.

The average annual salary for range managers working for the federal government is $34,082.

Additional Sources of Information

Bureau of Land Management
U.S. Department of the Interior
Room 3619
1849 C Street, NW
Washington, DC 20240

Society for Range Management
1839 York Street
Denver, CO 80206

Rehabilitation Counselor

The Job   Rehabilitation counselors work with mentally, physically, and emotionally disabled persons to help them become self-sufficient and productive. Many counselors specialize in one type of disability, such as the mentally retarded, the mentally ill, or the blind.

In the course of designing an individual rehabilitation program, the counselor may consult doctors, teachers, and family members to determine the client's abilities and the exact nature of the handicap or disability. He or she will, of course, also work closely with the client, arrange specialized training and specific job-related training, and provide encouragement and emotional support.

An important part of a counselor's work is finding employers who will hire the disabled and the handicapped. Many counselors keep in touch with members of the local business community and try to convince them to provide jobs for the disabled. Once a person is placed in a job, the rehabilitation counselor keeps track of the daily progress of the employee and also confers with the employer about job performance and progress.

The amount of time spent with an individual client depends on the severity of the person's problems and the size of the counselor's case load. Counselors in private organizations can usually spend more time with their clients than those who work for state and local agencies. Less experienced counselors and counselors who work with the severely disabled usually handle the fewest cases at one time.

Most rehabilitation counselors are employed by state or local rehabilitation agencies. Others work in hospitals or sheltered workshops or are employed by insurance companies and labor unions. The Department of Veterans Affairs employs psychologists who act as rehabilitation counselors.

Places of Employment and Working Conditions   Rehabilitation counselors work throughout the country, with the largest concentrations in metropolitan areas.

A 40-hour workweek is usual, but attendance at community meetings sometimes requires extra hours. A counselor's working hours are not entirely spent in the office and include trips to prospective employers, training agencies, and clients' homes.

The work of a counselor can be emotionally exhausting and sometimes discouraging.

Qualifications, Education, and Training   Anyone considering this field should have emotional stability, the ability to accept responsibility and

to work independently, and the ability to motivate and guide other people. Patience is also a necessary trait for a rehabilitation counselor because progress often comes slowly over a long period of time.

High school courses in the social sciences should be a part of a college preparatory course.

A bachelor's degree with a major in education, psychology, guidance, or sociology is the minimum requirement. This is sufficient for only a few entry-level jobs.

Advanced degrees in psychology, vocational counseling, or rehabilitation counseling are necessary for almost all jobs in this field.

Most rehabilitation counselors work for state and local government agencies and are required to pass the appropriate civil service examinations before appointment to a position. Many private organizations require counselors to be certified; this is achieved by passing the examinations administered by the Commission on Rehabilitation Counselor Certification.

Potential and Advancement   Job opportunities are expected to be very good, as employment in this field is expected to grow faster than the average for all occupations through the year 2005. There will be more people needing rehabilitation because advances in medical technology save lives that only a short time ago would have been lost.

Experienced rehabilitation counselors can advance to supervisory and administrative jobs.

Income   Median earnings for counselors are about $31,000 a year. Those in the middle of the salary range earn between $24,200 and $40,000 a year; the bottom 10 percent of the range earn less than $17,700; and the top 10 percent of the range earn over $49,300.

Additional Sources of Information

National Council on Rehabilitation Education
1213 29th Street, NW
Washington, DC 20007

National Rehabilitation Counseling Association
633 South Washington Street
Alexandria, VA 22314

Secret Service Agent

The Job   The U.S. Secret Service is part of the Department of the Treasury and employs special agents and uniformed officers.

Special agents have both protective and investigative responsibilities. Their primary responsibility is the protection of the president of the United States. They also protect the vice-president, the president-elect and vice-president elect, a former president and his wife, the widow of a former president until her death or remarriage, minor children of a former president until age 16, major presidential and vice-presidential candidates, and visiting heads of foreign states or foreign governments.

Special agents also work to suppress counterfeiting of U.S. currency and securities, and investigate and arrest people involved in forging and cashing government checks, bonds, and securities. All special agents must qualify for both protective and investigative assignments.

The Secret Service Uniformed division employs uniformed officers to provide protection for the president and his immediate family while they are in residence at the White House. Previously called the White House Police, their duties have been expanded to include protection of the vice-president and his immediate family, the White House and grounds, the official residence of the vice-president in Washington, D.C., buildings in which presidential offices are located, and foreign diplomatic missions located in the metropolitan Washington, D.C., area or other such areas of U.S. territories and possessions as the president may direct.

Uniformed officers carry out their responsibilities through foot and vehicular patrols, fixed posts, and canine teams.

Treasury security force officers are also a part of the Secret Service Uniformed division. They are responsible for security at the main treasury building and the treasury annex and for security of the office of the secretary of the treasury. They have investigative and special arrest powers in connection with laws violated within the treasury building including forgery and fraudulent negotiation or redemption of government checks, bonds, and securities.

Places of Employment and Working Conditions   Special agents may be employed at Secret Service headquarters in Washington, D.C., or at one of over 100 field offices and residential agencies throughout the United States. Uniformed officers and treasury security force officers work in Washington, D.C.

Special agents must be willing to work wherever they are assigned and are subject to frequent reassignment. Because the protective responsibilities of the Secret Service continue around the clock, all agents and officers perform some shift work.

Qualifications, Education, and Training   Each of these three Secret Service jobs has separate physical and educational requirements. All, however, require a comprehensive background investigation and top-secret security clearance.

Applicants for special agent appointments must be less than 35 years of age at the time of entrance to duty; be in excellent physical condition and pass a rigorous medical examination; have weight in proportion to height; and distance vision, uncorrected, of 20/20 in one eye and no less than 20/30 in the other.

Applicants must have a bachelor's degree in any major field of study or three years' experience of which at least two are in criminal investigation or a comparable combination of experience and education. A passing grade on the Treasury Enforcement Agent Examination, administered by area offices of the United States Civil Service Commission, is a prerequisite for consideration.

Only a limited number of the most qualified applicants reach the interview stage. They are rated on personal appearance, bearing and manner, ability to speak logically and effectively, and ability to adapt easily to a variety of situations. Applicants who achieve appointment must be prepared to wait an extended period of time for a vacancy to occur; it is usually during this period that background investigations are completed.

Once active duty begins, special agents receive general investigative training at the Federal Law Enforcement Training Center in Brunswick, Georgia, and specialized training at Secret Service facilities in Washington, D.C. They study protective techniques, criminal law, investigative procedures and devices, document and handwriting examination and analysis, first aid, use of firearms, and arrest techniques. They also receive on-the-job training. Advanced in-service training programs continue throughout an agent's career.

Uniformed officers must be U.S. citizens, have vision of at least 20/40 in each eye (correctable to 20/20), have weight in proportion to height, and pass a comprehensive physical examination. They must have a high school diploma or equivalent of one year of experience as a police officer in a city of over 500,000 population. Applicants must pass a written examination and an in-depth personal interview and have a valid driver's license.

Uniformed officers undergo a period of training at Secret Service facilities in Beltsville, Maryland, and Brunswick, Georgia. They study legal procedures in law enforcement, first aid, community relations, self-defense, and the use and care of firearms. Additional on-the-job training takes place after assignment.

Potential and Advancement   From time to time the service may actively recruit for a specific job category, but, for the most part, job opportunities are limited. The extremely high public interest in this work means that only the most highly qualified applicants are considered for appointment. Even after that acceptance, special agents must wait until a vacancy occurs before they begin active service.

Promotion depends on performance and the needs of the Secret Service.

Income   Special agents start at about $17,000 or $21,000 a year. Experienced agents start at $37,300, and supervisory agents start at $44,300.

Additional Sources of Information

The nearest area office of the U.S. Civil Service Commission can supply information on examination schedules. Also, contact any Office of Personnel Management Job Information Center for pamphlets that provide general information on Secret Service and Treasury Department jobs.

Social Worker

The Job   Social workers strive to help individuals, families, groups, and communities solve their problems. They also work to increase and improve the community resources available to people.

Depending on the nature of the problem and the time and resources available for solving it, social workers may choose one of three approaches or a combination of them—casework, group work, or community organization.

In casework, social workers interview individuals or families to identify problems. They help people understand and solve their problems by securing appropriate social resources such as financial aid, education, job training, or medical assistance.

In group work, social workers work with people in groups, helping them to understand one another. They plan and conduct activities for children, teenagers, adults, older people, and other groups in community centers, hospitals, and nursing homes.

In community organizations, social workers coordinate the work of political, civic, religious, and business groups working to combat social problems. They help plan and develop health, housing, welfare, and recreation services.

Many social workers provide direct social services, working for public and voluntary agencies such as state and local departments of public assistance and community welfare and religious organizations. Others work for schools, hospitals, business, and industry. Some social workers are in private practice and provide counseling services on a fee basis.

Places of Employment and Working Conditions

Social workers are employed throughout the United States, usually in urban areas.

Most social workers have a 5-day, 35- to 40-hour workweek. Evening and weekend work are sometimes necessary.

Qualifications, Education, and Training

A social worker must be sensitive, have concern for the needs of others, be objective and emotionally stable, and be willing to handle responsibility.

A college preparatory course in high school should provide as broad a background as possible. Volunteer work or a part-time or summer job in a community center, camp, or social welfare agency provide good experience.

A bachelor's degree in social work (B.S.W.) or a major in sociology or psychology can prepare the student for positions in this field, but the usual requirement is a master's degree in social work (M.S.W.). Those with only a bachelor's degree have limited promotion opportunities.

The M.S.W. degree is awarded after two years of specialized study and supervised field instruction. A graduate degree plus experience are necessary for supervisory and administrative positions; research work also requires training in social science research methods.

A Ph.D. is usually required for teaching and for top administrative positions.

The National Association of Social Workers (NASW) grants certifications and the title *ACSW* (Academy of Certified Social Workers) to members who qualify.

Forty-eight states and the District of Columbia require the licensing, certification, or registration of social workers. Requirements usually include specified experience plus an examination. Social workers employed by federal, state, and local government agencies are usually required to pass a civil service test before appointment to a position.

Potential and Advancement

There are about 438,000 social workers. Job opportunities should be plentiful through the year 2005; employment is expected to increase faster than the average for all occupations. This is due to the rapidly growing elderly population, the concern for the mentally ill and mentally retarded, and the need to replace social workers who leave the field.

Advancement in this field depends on experience and advanced education.

Income   Social workers employed by the federal government earn an average of $38,195 a year. Social workers in all other types of settings earn between $23,000 and $36,000 a year.

Additional Sources of Information

Council on Social Work Education
1600 Duke Street
Alexandria, VA 22314

National Association of Social Workers
7981 Eastern Avenue
Silver Spring, MD 20910

Sociologist

The Job   Sociologists study human social behavior by examining the groups that human beings form—from families, tribes, and governments to social, religious, and political organizations. Some sociologists study the characteristics of social groups and institutions; others study the way individuals are affected by the groups to which they belong.

Sociologists typically specialize in an area such as criminology, racial and ethnic relations, urban studies, or household and family matters. Their research helps lawmakers, educators, and administrators in their efforts to resolve social problems and formulate public policy.

The federal government employs sociologists in the departments of Health and Human Services, Agriculture, Interior, and Defense. Their work includes performing research and offering advice on such issues as poverty, crime, public assistance, population growth, education, mental health, racial and ethnic relations, drug abuse, and school dropouts.

Places of Employment and Working Conditions   Sociologists must do a great deal of reading, research, and writing. Those who work for the federal government have structured work schedules, and they sometimes face the pressures of deadlines, heavy work loads, and overtime. Some travel may be required to perform research or attend professional conferences.

Qualifications, Education, and Training
Study and research skills are necessary as well as strong communication skills.

In high school, a college preparatory course with a strong academic program is the best background.

A master's degree with a major in sociology is usually the minimum requirement in this field. A Ph.D. is required for directors of major research projects and for important administrative positions.

The federal government generally requires entry-level workers to have a college degree with 24 semester hours in sociology, including courses in theory and methods of social research. Those with advanced degrees will have an advantage, because competition is keen for the limited number of positions in this field.

Potential and Advancement
Sociologists should find employment opportunities as the demand for research in fields such as gerontology, criminology, and demography increases. Most job openings will occur, however, to replace those who leave the field.

Opportunities will be best for those with advanced degrees.

Advancement in this field depends on experience and obtaining higher degrees.

Income
Sociologists with a bachelor's degree can earn starting salaries of $17,000 or $21,000 a year with the federal government; those with a master's start at about $25,700; and those with a Ph.D., $31,100 or $37,300. The annual earnings of sociologists working for the federal government average about $49,600.

Additional Sources of Information

The American Sociological Association
1722 N Street, NW
Washington, DC 20036

Soil Conservationist

The Job Soil conservationists provide technical advice to farmers, ranchers, and others on soil and water conservation as well as land erosion. They design programs that will result in the most productive use of land without damaging it. They visit areas suffering from land erosion, determine what is causing it, and advise landowners on the best methods of controlling it.

Most soil conservationists are employed by the federal government in the Department of Agriculture's Soil Conservation Service or the Department of Interior's Bureau of Land Management. Other soil conservationists work for state and local governments.

Places of Employment and Working Conditions Soil conservationists work throughout the United States in nearly every county.

Conservationists work both indoors in labs and outdoors in all kinds of weather conditions. Their work can be physically demanding, and they are sometimes required to travel to remote areas by airplane, helicopters, four-wheel vehicles, and horses.

Qualifications, Education, and Training A soil conservationist should have good communication skills, an analytical mind, and a liking for outdoor work.

High school courses should include chemistry and biology.

Soil conservationists usually have a bachelor's degree with a major in agronomy (interaction of plants and soils), agricultural education, general agriculture, or related fields of natural resource sciences such as wildlife biology or forestry. Courses in agricultural engineering and cartography are also helpful.

An advanced degree is usually necessary for research positions.

Potential and Advancement This field is expected to grow more slowly than the average for all occupations through the year 2005. The number of applicants will continue to exceed the number of job openings with the federal government.

Advancement is limited. Conservationists working at the county level can move up to state and then national positions.

Income   Starting annual salaries with the federal government are $16,973 or $21,023 with a bachelor's degree and $21,023 or $25,717 with a master's degree. Those with Ph.D.s start at $31,116 or $37,294.

The average salary for soil conservationists employed by the federal government is $35,835.

Additional Sources of Information

Soil Conservation Service
U.S. Department of Agriculture
14th Street and Independence Avenue, SW
Washington, DC 20013

Soil Scientist

The Job   Soil scientists study the physical, chemical, biological, and behavioral characteristics of soils. Their work is important to farmers, builders, fertilizer manufacturers, real estate appraisers, and lending institutions.

A large part of soil science has to do with categorizing soils according to a national classification system. Once the soils in an area have been classified, the soil scientist prepares a map that shows soil types throughout the area.

A builder who wants to erect a factory or an apartment building will consult a soil-type map to locate a spot with a secure base of firm soils. Farmers also consult soil-type maps. Some communities require a certified soil scientist to examine the soil and test the drainage capabilities of any building lot that will be used with a septic system.

Some soil scientists conduct research into the chemical and biological properties of soil to determine what crops grow best in which soils. They test fertilizers and soils to determine ways to improve less productive soils. Soil scientists are also involved in pollution control programs and soil erosion prevention programs.

More than half of all soil scientists are employed by the Soil Conservation Service of the U.S. Department of Agriculture. Others are employed by state governments at agricultural experiment stations or agricultural colleges. Local governments also employ soil scientists.

Places of Employment and Working Conditions Soil scientists work in every state and in most counties of the United States.

They spend much of their time doing fieldwork in a particular area—usually a county. During bad weather they work indoors preparing maps and writing reports. Soil scientists involved in research usually work in greenhouses or small farm fields.

Qualifications, Education, and Training An interest in science and agriculture is necessary as well as a liking for outdoor work. Writing skills are also important.

High school courses should include chemistry and biology.

A bachelor's degree with a major in soil science or a closely related field such as agriculture or agronomy (interaction of plants and soils) is necessary. Courses in chemistry and cartography (mapmaking) are also important.

An advanced degree is necessary for many better paying research positions.

Some states require certification of soil scientists who inspect soil conditions prior to building or highway construction. Certification usually entails a written examination plus specified combinations of education and experience.

Potential and Advancement Job opportunities should be good for soil scientists through the year 2005 because of a decline in the number of graduates in this field and because employment is expected to grow faster than the average for all occupations. However, employment in federal agencies is not expected to grow much due to budget cuts.

Soil scientists who have been trained in both fieldwork and laboratory research will have the best opportunities for advancement, especially if they have an advanced degree.

Income The average salary for soil scientists employed by the federal government is $39,216 a year.

Additional Sources of Information

American Society of Agronomy
Crop Science Society of America
Soil Science Society of America
677 South Segoe Road
Madison, WI 53711

Soil Conservation Service
14th Street and Independence Avenue, SW
Washington, DC 20013

Statistician

The Job Statisticians gather and interpret numerical data and apply their knowledge of statistical methods to a particular subject area such as economics, human behavior, natural science, or engineering. They may predict population growth, develop quality control tests for manufactured products, or help business managers and government officials make decisions and evaluate programs.

Statisticians often obtain information about a group of people or things by surveying a portion of the whole. They decide where to gather the data, determine the size and type of the sample group, and develop the survey questionnaire or reporting form. Statisticians who design experiments prepare mathematical models to test a particular theory. Those in analytical work interpret collected data and prepare tables, charts, and written reports on their findings. Mathematical statisticians use mathematical theory to design and improve statistical methods.

The federal government employs statisticians, primarily in the departments of Commerce (Bureau of the Census), Agriculture, and Health and Human Services. Statisticians are also employed by state and local governments.

Qualifications, Education, and Training Statisticians must have good reasoning ability, persistence, and the ability to apply principles to new types of problems.

High school courses in mathematics are important.

A bachelor's degree with a major in statistics or mathematics is the minimum requirement for this field. A bachelor's degree with a major in a related field such as economics or natural science with a minor in statistics is preferred for some jobs. The federal government requires entry-level statisticians to have a college degree, including at least 15 hours of statistics or a combination of 15 hours of mathematics and statistics with at least six semester hours in statistics. An additional nine hours in another academic discipline are also required.

Many jobs require graduate work in mathematics or statistics, and courses in computer use and techniques are becoming increasingly important. Economics and business administration courses are also helpful.

Potential and Advancement   Although this employment field is expected to have slow growth through the year 2005, there will be job opportunities. There will be a demand in the federal government for statisticians in fields such as agriculture, demography, consumer and producer surveys, transportation, Social Security, health, education, energy conservation, and environmental quality control. Those with advanced degrees will have more opportunities; there will be a great deal of competition for entry-level jobs for those with only the minimum qualifications.

Opportunities for promotion in this field are best for those with advanced degrees. Experienced statisticians may advance to positions of greater technical responsibility and to supervisory positions.

Income   The average salary for all statisticians employed by the federal government is $47,618 a year; mathematical statisticians earn, on average, $48,427.

Additional Sources of Information

American Statistical Association
1429 Duke Street
Alexandria, VA 22314

Surveyor

The Job   Surveyors measure construction sites, establish official land boundaries, assist in setting land valuations, and collect information for maps and charts.

Most surveyors serve as leaders of surveying teams; they are in charge of the field party and responsible for the accuracy of its work. They record the information disclosed by the survey; verify the accuracy of the survey data; and prepare the sketches, maps, and reports.

A typical field party consists of the party chief and three to six assistants and helpers. Instrument workers adjust and operate surveying instruments and compile notes. Chain workers use steel tape or surveyor's chain to measure distances between surveying points; they usually work in pairs and may mark measured points with stakes. Rod workers use a level rod, range pole, or other equipment to assist instrument workers in determining elevations, distances, and directions. They hold and move the range pole according to hand or voice signals from the instrument worker and remove underbrush from the survey line.

Surveyors often specialize in highway surveys; land surveys to establish boundaries (these are also required for the preparation of maps and legal descriptions for deeds and leases); or topographic surveys to determine elevations, depressions, and contours and the location of roads, rivers, and buildings. Other specialties are mining, pipeline, gravity, and magnetic surveying.

Photogrammetrists measure and interpret photographs to determine various characteristics of natural or artificial features of an area. They apply analytical processes and mathematical techniques to aerial, space, ground, and underwater photographs to prepare detailed maps of areas that are inaccessible or difficult to survey. Control surveys on the ground are then made to determine the accuracy of the maps derived from photogrammetric techniques.

Federal, state, and local government agencies employ about one-quarter of all surveyors. Those who work for state and local governments usually work for highway departments and urban planning and development agencies. Those who work for the federal government are in the U.S. Geological Survey, the Bureau of Land Management, the Army Corps of Engineers, the Forest Service, the National Ocean Survey, and the Defense Mapping Agency.

Places of Employment and Working Conditions   Surveyors work throughout the United States.

Surveying is outdoor work, and surveyors often walk long distances or climb hills carrying equipment and instruments. They usually work an eight-hour, five-day week but may work longer hours in summer months when conditions are more favorable for surveying.

Qualifications, Education, and Training   Surveyors should be in good physical condition. They need good eyesight, coordination, and hearing and must have the ability to visualize and understand objects, distances, sizes, and other abstract forms. They also need mathematical ability.

High school courses should include algebra, geometry, trigonometry, drafting, and mechanical drawing.

Surveyors acquire their skills through a combination of on-the-job training and courses in surveying. Technical institutes, vocational schools, and junior colleges offer one- , two- , and three-year programs in surveying.

High school graduates without any training usually start as helpers. If they complete a surveying course and gain experience, they may advance to technician, senior survey technician, party chief, and, finally, licensed surveyor.

Photogrammetrists usually need a bachelor's degree in engineering or the physical sciences.

All states require the licensing or registration of land surveyors. Registration requirements are very strict because, once registered, surveyors can be held legally responsible for their work. Requirements usually include formal education courses and from five to twelve years of surveying experience.

Potential and Advancement Job opportunities are expected to grow steadily in this field. Openings will result from a growing demand for surveyors as well as from workers who leave the field or transfer to other occupations. An anticipated growth in construction through the year 2005 will also contribute to this increased demand.

Advancement in this field depends primarily on accumulating experience.

Income Surveyors in entry-level jobs with little or no experience or training earn about $12,385 a year working for the federal government; with one year of related postsecondary training, $13,515; with an associate degree that includes courses in surveying, $15,171.

The average annual salary for land surveyors employed by the federal government is $37,024.

Additional Sources of Information

American Congress on Surveying and Mapping
5410 Grosvenor Lane
Bethesda, MD 20814-2122

American Society for Photogrammetry and Remote Sensing
5410 Grosvenor Lane
Suite 200
Bethesda, MD 20814

Systems Analyst

The Job Systems analysts decide what new data need to be collected, the equipment needed to process the data, and the procedure to be followed in using the information within any given computer system. They use various techniques such as cost accounting, sampling, and mathematical model building to analyze a problem and devise a new system to solve it.

Once a system has been developed, the systems analyst prepares charts and diagrams that describe the system's operation in terms that the manager or customer who will use the system can understand. The analyst may also prepare a cost-benefit analysis of the newly developed system. If the system is accepted, the systems analyst then translates the logical requirements of the system into the capabilities of the particular computer machinery (hardware) in use and prepares specifications for programmers to follow. The systems analyst will also work with the programmers to debug (eliminate errors from) a new system.

Because the work is complex and varied, systems analysts specialize in either business or scientific and engineering applications. Some analysts improve systems already in use or adapt existing systems to handle additional types of data. Those involved in research, called advanced systems designers, devise new methods of analysis.

Most systems analysts employed by the federal government work in the departments of the Treasury, Defense, and Health and Human Services; however, nearly every government agency employs systems analysts.

Sometimes systems analysts begin as computer programmers and are promoted to analyst positions only after gaining experience. In large data processing departments, they may start as junior systems analysts. Many persons enter this occupation after experience in accounting, economics, business management, or engineering.

Places of Employment and Working Conditions   Opportunities for systems analysts exist throughout the entire country.

Systems analysts usually work a normal 40-hour week with occasional evening or weekend work.

Qualifications, Education, and Training   Systems analysts must be able to think logically, concentrate, and handle abstract ideas. They must be able to communicate effectively with technical personnel such as programmers as well as those who have no computer background.

High school should include as many mathematics and computer courses as possible.

Because job requirements vary so greatly, there is no universally accepted way of preparing for a career as a systems analyst. A background in accounting, business administration, or economics is preferred by some employers. Courses in computer concepts, systems analysis, and data retrieval techniques are good preparation for any systems analyst.

Many employers require a college degree in computer science, information science, or data processing. Scientifically oriented organizations often require graduate work as well as a combination of computer science and a science or engineering specialty.

Because technical advances in the computer field come so rapidly, systems analysts must continue their technical education throughout their careers. This training usually takes the form of one- and two-week courses offered by employers, computer manufacturers, and software (computer systems) vendors.

The Institute for Certification of Computer Professionals confers the designation of *certified data processor* (CDP) on systems analysts who have five years of experience and who successfully complete a core examination and exams in two specialty areas.

Potential and Advancement   This job field is expected to grow steadily because of the expanding use of computers and the need to use them as efficiently as possible. College graduates who have had courses in computer programming, systems analysis, and data processing will have the best opportunities, while those without a degree may face some competition for the available jobs that don't require a degree.

Systems analysts can advance to jobs as lead systems analysts or managers of systems analysis or data processing departments.

Income   Entry-level salaries for college graduates employed by the federal government are about $17,000 or $21,000 a year, depending on academic records.

Additional Sources of Information

Association for Systems Management
24587 Bagley Road
Cleveland, OH 44138

Institute for the Certification of Computer Professionals
2200 East Devon Avenue
Suite 268
Des Plaines, IL 60018

Translator

The Job   Translators render the written material of one language into written material in another language. Their work differs from that of interpreters, who provide oral translation.

The largest single employer of translators is the U.S. government. Agencies such as the Joint Publications Research Service have in-house translation staffs, while other government agencies contract their translating requirements to commercial translating agencies, which in turn employ free-lancers. Most translators work on a free-lance basis.

Places of Employment and Working Conditions   The largest concentrations of translators are in the New York City and Washington, D.C., areas, where government and publishing industry requirements provide the most job opportunities.

Working conditions vary from an office setting to the free-lancer's own home. Occasionally, a rush assignment may mean long or irregular working hours, but in-house translators usually work a 37- to 40-hour week. Free-lance translators can set their own schedules. Many work only part-time—some through choice, but many because they cannot secure enough free-lance work to provide a steady income.

Qualifications, Education, and Training   Translators need a working knowledge of one or more foreign languages. A translator's own foreign background, time spent living abroad, or intensive study of a language at the college or university level provides sufficient preparation for many translating jobs.

A college degree is usually necessary for this type of work. Course work should include foreign languages and writing. Studying abroad can also be a very valuable experience for translators.

Potential and Advancement   There are fewer than 2,000 translators working full-time in the United States. Exact numbers are difficult because those employed full-time, as well as those handling only an occasional assignment in conjunction with other work, are all classed as translators. Job opportu-

nities in this field are limited, since any full-time, in-house positions are usually filled from the existing pool of free-lancers.

Advancement in this field usually takes the form of better translating assignments because of experience and reputation. Some translators form their own commercial translating agencies and secure contract work for themselves and their in-house or free-lance staff.

Income Beginning translators earn about $18,000 a year. Free-lance translators may charge by the word or by the hour. Some free-lance translators earn between $15 and $30 an hour.

Additional Sources of Information

American Translators Association
109 Croton Avenue
Ossining, NY 10562

Institute of International Education
809 United Nations Plaza
New York, NY 10017

Translators and Interpreters Educational Society
P.O. Box 3027
Stanford, CA 94305

Urban Planner

The Job Urban planners develop plans and programs to provide for the future growth of a community; revitalize run-down areas of a community; and achieve more efficient uses of the community's land, social services, industry, and transportation.

Before preparing plans or programs, urban planners conduct detailed studies of local conditions and current population. After preparing a plan, they develop cost estimates and other relevant materials and aid in the presentation of the program before community officials, planning boards, and citizens' groups.

Most urban planners (also called city planners, community planners, or regional planners) work for city, county, or regional planning agencies. State and federal agencies employ urban planners in the fields of housing, transportation, and environmental protection.

Many urban planners do consulting work, either part-time or in addition to a regular job or full-time for firms that provide planning services to government agencies.

Places of Employment and Working Conditions
Urban planners are employed throughout the United States in communities of all sizes.

A 40-hour workweek is usual for urban planners, but evening and weekend hours are often necessary for meetings and community activities.

Qualifications, Education, and Training
The ability to analyze relationships and to visualize plans and designs is necessary for urban planners. They should be able to work well with people and cooperate with those who may have different viewpoints.

High school students interested in this field should take social science and mathematics courses. Part-time or summer jobs in community government offices can be helpful.

Almost all jobs in this field require a master's degree in urban and regional planning, even for entry-level positions. Most graduate programs require two years to complete. Part-time or summer work in a planning office is usually a required part of the advanced degree program.

Urban planners seeking employment with federal, state, or local governments usually must pass civil service examinations before securing a position.

Potential and Advancement
There are about 23,000 urban planners at work in the United States. This field is expected to grow through the year 2005, but demand for urban planners will be greater in some regions than in others. Demand for urban planners will be higher in states such as Florida and Maine, which have mandated planning, and in rapidly growing areas. There will also be many opportunities in smaller cities and in older areas, like the Northeast, which are undergoing development and preservation.

Income
Salaries for urban planners vary according to degree, employer, experience, size of community for which they work, and geographic location.

Urban planners employed at the various levels of government earn the following median annual salaries: city governments, $38,000; county governments, $34,700; joint city/county governments, $32,400; and state governments, $40,000. Urban and regional planners employed by the federal government earn an average annual salary of $48,000.

Additional Sources of Information

American Planning Association
1776 Massachusetts Avenue, NW
Washington, DC 20036

Association of Collegiate Schools of Planning
Department of Urban Planning
University of Wisconsin
P.O. Box 413
Milwaukee, WI 53201

VGM CAREER BOOKS/CAREERS FOR YOU

OPPORTUNITIES IN

Accounting
Acting
Advertising
Aerospace
Agriculture
Airline
Animal and Pet Care
Architecture
Automotive Service
Banking
Beauty Culture
Biological Sciences
Biotechnology
Book Publishing
Broadcasting
Building Construction Trades
Business Communication
Business Management
Cable Television
CAD/CAM
Carpentry
Chemistry
Child Care
Chiropractic
Civil Engineering
Cleaning Service
Commercial Art and Graphic Design
Computer Maintenance
Computer Science
Counseling & Development
Crafts
Culinary
Customer Service
Data Processing
Dental Care
Desktop Publishing
Direct Marketing
Drafting
Electrical Trades
Electronic and Electrical Engineering
Electronics
Energy
Engineering
Engineering Technology
Environmental
Eye Care
Fashion
Fast Food
Federal Government
Film
Financial
Fire Protection Services
Fitness
Food Services
Foreign Language
Forestry
Government Service
Health and Medical
High Tech
Home Economics
Homecare Services
Hospital Administration
Hotel & Motel Management
Human Resources Management
  Careers
Information Systems
Insurance
Interior Design
International Business
Journalism
Laser Technology
Law
Law Enforcement and Criminal
  Justice
Library and Information Science
Machine Trades
Magazine Publishing

Marine & Maritime
Masonry
Marketing
Materials Science
Mechanical Engineering
Medical Imaging
Medical Technology
Metalworking
Microelectronics
Military
Modeling
Music
Newspaper Publishing
Nonprofit Organizations
Nursing
Nutrition
Occupational Therapy
Office Occupations
Packaging Science
Paralegal Careers
Paramedical Careers
Part-time & Summer Jobs
Performing Arts
Petroleum
Pharmacy
Photography
Physical Therapy
Physician
Plastics
Plumbing & Pipe Fitting
Postal Service
Printing
Property Management
Psychology
Public Health
Public Relations
Purchasing
Real Estate
Recreation and Leisure
Refrigeration and Air Conditioning
Religious Service
Restaurant
Retailing
Robotics
Sales
Secretarial
Securities
Social Science
Social Work
Speech-Language Pathology
Sports & Athletics
Sports Medicine
State and Local Government
Teaching
Technical Communications
Telecommunications
Television and Video
Theatrical Design & Production
Tool and Die
Transportation
Travel
Trucking
Veterinary Medicine
Visual Arts
Vocational and Technical
Warehousing
Waste Management
Welding
Word Processing
Writing
Your Own Service Business

CAREERS IN Accounting; Advertising;
Business; Communications; Computers;
Education; Engineering; Finance;
Health Care; High Tech; Law;
Marketing; Medicine; Science; Social
and Rehabilitation Services

CAREER DIRECTORIES

Careers Encyclopedia
Dictionary of Occupational Titles
Occupational Outlook Handbook

CAREER PLANNING

Admissions Guide to Selective
  Business Schools
Beginning Entrepreneur
Career Planning and Development
  for College Students and Recent
  Graduates
Careers Checklists
Careers for Animal Lovers
Careers for Bookworms
Careers for Computer Buffs
Careers for Crafty People
Careers for Culture Lovers
Careers for Environmental Types
Careers for Film Buffs
Careers for Foreign Language
  Aficionados
Careers for Good Samaritans
Careers for Gourmets
Careers for Nature Lovers
Careers for Numbers Crunchers
Careers for Sport Nuts
Careers for Travel Buffs
Cover Letters They Don't Forget
Guide to Basic Resume Writing
How to Approach an Advertising Agency
  and Walk Away with the Job You Want
How to Bounce Back Quickly After
  Losing Your Job
How to Change Your Career
How to Choose the Right Career
How to Get and Keep
  Your First Job
How to Get into the Right Law School
How to Get People to Do Things
  Your Way
How to Have a Winning Job Interview
How to Jump Start a Stalled Career
How to Land a Better Job
How to Launch Your Career in
  TV News
How to Make the Right Career Moves
How to Market Your College Degree
How to Move from College into a
  Secure Job
How to Negotiate the Raise
  You Deserve
How to Prepare a *Curriculum Vitae*
How to Prepare for College
How to Run Your Own Home Business
How to Succeed in College
How to Succeed in High School
How to Write a Winning Resume
How to Write Your College
  Application Essay
Joyce Lain Kennedy's Career Book
Resumes for Advertising Careers
Resumes for Banking and Financial
  Careers
Resumes for College Students &
  Recent Graduates
Resumes for Communications Careers
Resumes for Education Careers
Resumes for Health and Medical Careers
Resumes for High School Graduates
Resumes for High Tech Careers
Resumes for Midcareer Job Changes
Resumes for Sales and Marketing Careers
Resumes for Scientific and Technical
  Careers
Successful Interviewing for College
  Seniors

VGM Career Horizons
a division of *NTC Publishing Group*
4255 West Touhy Avenue
Lincolnwood, Illinois 60646 1975